THE SEEKING HEART

A Journey with Henri Nouwen

Charles R. Ringma

PARACLETE PRESS
BREWSTER, MASSACHUSETTS

The Seeking Heart: A Journey With Henri Nouwen

2006 First Printing

ISBN 10: 1-55725-446-X
ISBN 13: 978-1-55725-446-7

　　Library of Congress Cataloging-in-Publication Data
Ringma, Charles.
　　The seeking heart : a journey with Henri Nouwen / by Charles R. Ringma.
　　　p. cm.
　　Includes bibliographical references.
　　ISBN 1-55725-446-X
　　1. Spiritual life—Catholic Church. 2. Spirituality—Catholic
Church. 3. Nouwen, Henri J. M. I. Title.
　　BX2350.3.R56 2006
　　242—dc22

10 9 8 7 6 5 4 3 2 1

Published by Paraclete Press
Brewster, Massachusetts
www.paracletepress.com

Printed in the United States of America

For
Howard and Shirley Bentall

Pilgrims of faith on a long journey,
And sowers of the good seed of the Reign of God

Contents

Heart and Head
The Journey and Empowerment of Faith

Heart to Heart
The Wonderment and Responsibility of Friendship and Community

The Heart's True Home

Preface

THE PAST DAYS have been a most uncanny experience.

I am reading Henri Nouwen's *Sabbatical Journey: The Diary of His Final Year* in preparation for writing a meditational reader using some of the key insights from the writings of this most influential contemporary author on Christian spirituality. Several weeks after his last entry of August 30, 1996, Henri dies of a heart attack.

I am also on sabbatical from my work at Regent College, Vancouver, aware of my own aging and the vulnerability of human existence. Could this also be my final writing project?

What is particularly disconcerting is that the hopes for a quieter and more reflective existence expressed in Nouwen's diary resonate with my own desires. Nouwen was hoping to play a different role at the L'Arche Daybreak community so that he could give more time to prayer, reflection, and writing. My life is moving in a similar direction. His hopes were realized in death. Will mine be realized in life?

It is within the framework of the fundamental fragility and uncertainty of life that this reflective reader is written. But it is a frame that holds the picture of faith, hope, and gratitude. While vulnerability can lead to resentment or despair, it can also lead to the exploration of the inner caverns of the heart sculpted by God's grace and beneficence. This is not to suggest that fear is absent. Nor does it suggest that one rationalizes all the difficulties. But it is possible to be fragile and full of hope. One can be weak, physically and emotionally, yet vibrant in faith.

This reflective reader is about the ways of the seeking heart. It is about the inner life as the source and fountain for the way we live in the world. Heart matters.

We need to be attentive to our inner world, all the more so in a world that pulls us to focus on the outward, on activity, on productivity. But not only are the issues of the heart important, there are also the matters of the heart: the matters of loneliness and fulfillment, despair and hope, doubt and faith, turmoil and peace, darkness and light. The matters of the heart are basic and determinative for who we are, what we become, and what we do. This reader invites you to a new attentiveness to the way of the heart.

Those of you who are familiar with my earlier work, *Seek the Silences with Thomas Merton*, will recognize this book to be a companion volume. My thanks go to Regent College Board of Governors for the gift of a much-needed sabbatical and to Marina Ringma-McLaren for doing the computer work. Finally, this book is dedicated to two members of the church I attended while living and working in Canada. Howard and Shirley (now deceased) Bentall were instrumental in creating the Salsbury Society as part of Grandview Calvary Baptist Church, East Vancouver, serving the poor, those in major life crises, and political refugee claimants. They also brought into being the Rivendell Retreat Centre on Bowen Island, British Columbia, Canada.

This book has been enhanced by the careful editorial work of Robert Edmonson. It has been a joy to work with him. My further thanks go to Jon M. Sweeney for the book's final shape.

Introduction

THE INVITATION TO BECOME MORE ATTENTIVE to the way of the seeking heart is to go to the very core of many of the world's religious traditions. In these traditions the importance of solitude, meditation, prayer, faith, and hope are emphasized. These are heart matters.

In the Judeo-Christian tradition the heart is seen as the reflective and motivational center of the human person. In the pages of Scripture we find rich insights regarding the matters of the heart. "The LORD searches every mind" (1 Chr. 28:9). "Keep your heart with all vigilance, for from it flow the springs of life" (Prov. 4:23). "A new heart I will give you, and a new spirit I will put within you" (Ezek. 36:26). "Blessed are the pure in heart, for they will see God" (Mt. 5:8).

The way of the heart, therefore, has to do with what is fundamental to who we are. It has to do with what moves and motivates us. It has to do with our greatest passions. And since the issues of faith cannot be peripheral to who we are, but are to be central, faith and spirituality are heart matters. They lie at the very core of our identity.

It is for this reason that Jesus invites us to love God and our neighbor with all of our heart. For some the focus on heart matters suggests an unhealthy preoccupation with inwardness and introspection. And in some of the history of Christian spirituality this has occurred. At various times in the long history of Christianity, heart matters became only God matters, and the neighbor was lost from view. The soul became the focus while the body was neglected. Prayer became paramount, and loving concern for others was neglected. Heart matters, however, ought not to lead to a world-denying form of Christianity. The way of the heart is the way of love: a love of God and a love of creation, a love of spiritual renewal and of artistic beauty, a love of contemplation and the work for justice. Heart matters are all-of-life matters.

Because it is so easy for us to lose our way in the midst of life's activities and concerns, and become distracted, discouraged, and confused, it is important for us to guard our heart. Losing one's way can happen in every and any sphere of life. It is not only in the freneticism of work on the Stock Exchange or in the boredom of an unskilled job that one can become disconnected from the ways of the heart. This can also happen in the midst of religious activity.

One of my biggest challenges working in graduate Christian education is remaining attentive to the presence of God, the inspiration of the Holy Spirit, the need for solitude and reflection, the movement of prayer, and making responses to others born out of a love that frees and blesses. These are all matters of the heart, which so easily can become eroded or lost from view. It is for this reason that the focus of this book is on the way of the *seeking* heart. This recognizes movement at the very core of our existence rather than settledness. This is the sojourner motif.

The seeking heart is the restless heart. It is the hungry heart.

The habits of the heart envisaged in this reflective reader are not the disciplines of the safe, settled, and secure. Instead, they are the habits of the heart of one who knows how to cry, to lament, to be ecstatic, to search, to find, and to search again.

The seeking heart is the heart open to change, renewal, and conversion.

The above, I trust, will give you the reader, some hint of this book's direction. But a further important hint is called for. There are multiple layers of seeking reflected in this book. God's Spirit is seeking your wholeness and well-being as well as giving direction for your life. Nouwen, the author I interact with, was a man whose life was a restless seeking after God. I am seeking to challenge you, the reader, and myself to a deeper inwardness in order to be a more authentic and sacramental presence in the world. And you are seeking as well.

May we seek more deeply and, in so doing, live and serve more truly.

Introducing Henri Nouwen

HENRI NOUWEN WAS ONE OF THE MOST INFLUENTIAL WRITERS on Christian spirituality in the twentieth century.

His main appeal revolves around a range of key factors. Nouwen, though a Roman Catholic, was significantly ecumenical in his orientation. Nouwen, though a professional psychologist and theologian, was profoundly accessible to the general reader. Nouwen, though an apologist for the Christian faith, was deeply in touch with both the beauty and the pain of the human condition.

But while these factors all play a part, they don't quite, in my opinion, get to the heart of Nouwen's powerful appeal. Nouwen's appeal lies in his ability and willingness to write about the whole gamut of faith and life from a perspective of a vulnerable openness. While we learn of the faith of Nouwen, we also hear about his fears. While we hear about his certainties, we also get to know his doubts. While we become familiar with his gifts and passions, we are also exposed to his vulnerabilities and woundedness.

Nouwen, in a most amazing way, offered his very life in all of its spiritual, social, relational, vocational, and missional dimensions as a window through which the contemporary reader, whether believer or skeptic, may look for an embodied picture of what it means for a person to live the Christian life. As such, Nouwen is a witness to the gospel, to faith in Christ, to what a contemporary Christian might look like.

I am constantly surprised by the number of different people who have read some of the works of Henri Nouwen. It is almost as if Nouwen's voice has found resonance with all kinds of people. Psychologists have read his book *Intimacy*. Pastoral workers have appreciated *Creative Ministry* and his classic *The Wounded Healer*. Those involved in mission to the Third World have noted Nouwen's books *Compassion*, *Gracias*, and *Love in a Fearful Land*.

But Nouwen's writings have other audiences. There are works that specifically target a Roman Catholic audience. His *Clowning in Rome*, *Behold the Beauty of the Lord*, *Walk with Jesus*, and *Jesus and Mary* have this focus. There are books that are particularly helpful for those involved in church-related ministry. *In the Name of Jesus*, *The Living Reminder*, *Reaching Out*, and *The Way of the Heart* belong to this grouping of writings besides the already mentioned *Creative Ministry* and *The Wounded Healer*.

While some of Nouwen's books seem to have a more particular audience in view, his overall writing intent was to communicate with a general reader. And in this Nouwen was most successful. Many across Christian denominations, different religious traditions, and secular people seeking faith have turned to the writings of Nouwen.

What all have found most helpful is not only his recurring emphases on prayer, the practice of solitude, and the need for the contemplative experience in our busy and secular world. What has also been particularly helpful is Nouwen's willingness to share his life and struggles with regard to prayer, vocation, identity, sexuality, service, and witness. His *The Genesee Diary*, *The Road to Daybreak*, and *Sabbatical Journey* are outstanding examples of a form of writing that invites the reader into the very warp and woof of the writer's life. Nouwen's attempt to make his own life, with all of its faith and struggles, available to his readers is a wonderful form of witness and testimony to the raw realities of living the Christian life. Here vulnerability and humility sparkle rather than triumphalism. Here and in his other writings, one meets a fragile human being ever wrestling with his identity and security while being a priest, university lecturer, famous writer, and committed follower of Jesus Christ.

In my opinion, it is in these more autobiographical writings that the light of faith shines more clearly than in Nouwen's attempts at Christian apologetics in his *Letters to Marc about Jesus* and his *Life of the Beloved*

There are a number of important themes in the writings of Nouwen that I wish to highlight in this reflective reader, using key insights from Nouwen's prolific pen. The first and possibly the most basic is that Nouwen is a witness to the fact that life—no matter how vocationally successful—needs a faith basis to give it a framework, meaning, and passion.

Second, Nouwen constantly reminds us that the life of faith in Christ through the Spirit cannot be lived well without the spiritual disciplines of prayer, meditation, and contemplation as well as the practice of reading Scripture and participating in the Eucharistic life of a faith community.

Third, Nouwen proposes that the life of faith cannot be lived alone. It is life with God and with companions on the journey. It is life in community, never a life of "holy" isolation.

Fourth, and here Nouwen has been a tremendous challenge to the consumer Christianity that characterizes so much of the Western world, the life of faith in Christ is a life lived against the tide, against the idolatries of our culture. The life of faith is to be prophetic. And Nouwen has demonstrated that well in his critique of professionalism, his commitment to the poor, his embrace of vocational downward mobility.

Fifth, Nouwen's voice is an important reminder that the life of faith is a homecoming to the heart and an embrace of God, but this does not provide a final resolution. We live in a real world. We struggle with issues. Our healing is not complete. Therefore, the life of faith is always lived in faith. Sight awaits us in God's eschatological future.

Finally, although more could be said, the writings of Nouwen are an important witness to a humble, vulnerable, caring, loving form of Christianity. This may well continue to be an important witness in the decades to come as we see the older tribalisms re-emerge in our so-called multicultural world.

HEART
CRIES

The Beauty and Pain of the Human Condition

WHILE IN CHILDHOOD we take the world for granted and accept the gifts of parents, home, others, and the broader world around us, this innocence does not remain. We soon begin to realize that we have to take some position, some posture in relation to all that is around us. Our relationships and the world around us invite interaction and response.

The posture that we take in relation to the outer world depends a lot on what is happening in our inner world. If the inner house of our being is full of fear our response to the world will be one of suspicion. If the inner sanctum of the heart is full of love our response to the world will be one of joyful engagement.

But it is never just that simple. Our inner being is divided. Fear and love co-inhabit the inner house. So do faith and doubt, insecurity and control, love and resentment.

1

It is therefore appropriate to speak about heart cries. There is the frequently suppressed cry of boredom. There is the painful cry of the wounded heart. There is the infrequent cry of ecstasy and joy. Heart cries reflect attentiveness to the movement within our inner being. Heart cries are the ways of the heart.

This attentiveness is important. This inner contemplation is essential, for to the extent that we become deaf to the cries of our own heart, deaf to the heart cry of God, and inattentive to the cries of others and our world, to that extent a deadening narrowness will constrict the arteries of our being.

While heart cries also have to do with worship and prayer, in this first section our reflections will focus on the beauty and pain of the human condition, the refractory nature of our world, the ebb and flow of goodness and evil.

You may wonder whether this is a good place to start. Should we not begin in hope? Should we not start with God?

The answer to this is obvious. Yes, we should start in faith, and we will look at the ambivalent and complex nature of human existence from a theological perspective. But we don't want to go the way of denial. So often the Christian perspective is cast in escapist terms: Look to God and deny reality!

I wish to move in the opposite direction. We are in the world, we need to face it and fully live in it. This is what the doctrine of creation teaches us, and the incarnation of Jesus fully demonstrates Christian embodiment.

Henri Nouwen knew something about heart cries.

Not only in his book on prayer, *A Cry for Mercy*, but throughout his writings Nouwen revealed his struggles and his fragility. This is nowhere more clearly told than in his published journal of the time of his deepest crisis, *The Inner Voice of Love*. Here he speaks of his wounded self, his insecurities, and his insatiable need for love and affirmation. Writing about himself he says, "[F]or as long as you can remember, you have been a pleaser, depending on others to give you an identity" (p. 5). And elsewhere in the same book: "[T]here is a deep hole in your being, like an abyss. You will never succeed in filling that hole, because your needs are inexhaustible" (p. 3).

Even when our experience of life is marked by a dull uniformity, we all know something of the beauty and pain of human existence. Our inner world has its contradictions, while the outer world is marked by beneficence and injustice. And what we do to ourselves and to others, and what others do to us, is always a multi-textured reality sculpted by the most abundant grace and the greatest of stupidities. Both favor and folly are part of the human condition. Heart cries, however, can always be the genesis of healing.

Need's Cry
Drawing close to the only life giver

IT SHOULD NOT SURPRISE US that at the most basic level we are vulnerable and needy people. And it matters not that some of us may be financially well-to-do, politically powerful, and socially respectable.

While being needy is usually assigned to people with obvious difficulties, whether that be poverty, disability, marginality, or dysfunctionality, a sense of need pervades all of us. We experience ourselves as less than what we could be. And we all live with dimensions of brokenness and woundedness.

I am no different in this regard. My migrant experience has deeply marked me and left me with much insecurity.

Nor is Henri Nouwen an exception. All his life he looked for appreciation and affirmation from others.

But what this suggests is that all of our needs are not the same. In the First World, people's most basic need may be the search for significance. In the Third World, it may be the impulse toward economic survival and the search for justice.

At the more personal level this diversity also holds true. One person's most present pressing need may be meaningful relationships, another's may be health issues; a third person may be gripped by fear and a general sense of uselessness. As a result, our heart cries will be different as we have the courage to face our difficulties and areas of pain. And facing them is no light and easy matter. The flight into denial is ever at hand. The propensity to blame others is ever with us. And avoidance is primordial to the human condition.

But there are also needs that are common to all of us: Need for sustenance and for shelter. Need for love, protection, and care. Need for friendship and community. Need for meaningful work and activities.

It is important to realize that our needs are never one-dimensional. They are never just physical or economic. They are also spiritual. Thus our need for the embrace of God and our need for forgiveness and healing are as key to our well-being as our daily bread.

To whom do we turn with these our needs?

We can turn in the wrong direction. Sometimes we need to turn inward. Sometimes we need the humility to ask help from others. There are times when God alone can help us.

Henri Nouwen reminds us of this. He journals, "You have to move gradually from crying outward—crying out for people who you think can fulfill your needs—to crying inward to the place where you can let yourself be held and carried by God."[1] Some of our deepest needs cannot be met by others. And in our inappropriate demands on others we may destroy many a potential relationship. There are existential needs that can only be met by God's forgiveness, grace, and embrace.

Our deepest primordial longing comes from the flight from Eden. While we sought the "blessing" of human autonomy, we return unfulfilled and therefore need to quench our thirst in the welcome of the God who seeks us and longs to bring us home into the shelter of his benediction.

Enough
The cry for Sabbath

OURS HAS BECOME A STRANGE AND CONTRADICTORY WORLD. We are constantly promised much, but much eludes us. We are bombarded with messages of rest, relaxation, and the ultimate vacation, but we are working harder than ever, and our inner world knows more of turmoil than peace.

The orientation toward productivity, usefulness, achievement, success, and upward mobility has left us full of exhilaration as we respond to all the challenges before us, but has also left us deeply depleted and inwardly restless.

It seems that this state of affairs is not only the result of certain kinds of work associated with great levels of stress, such as law-enforcement, the stock exchange, air-traffic control. A deeper malaise has affected us all in every sphere of work, including religious and spiritual activities.

Henri Nouwen as a spiritual resource to those with physical and intellectual disabilities makes a familiar lament: He confesses, "I realize that sometimes I am tired of putting up another fight, waging another battle for the good. Sometimes I just want to be left alone."[2] There are many layers and contours to this most basic of complaints.

One has to do with the ambivalence we experience when the doing of good seems to make so little immediate difference. We pray, we serve, we disciple, we encourage. But there is so little to show for it. Another comes from the recognition that nothing comes about easily. There is hard work involved: Thinking. Visioning. Planning. Strategizing. Mobilizing. Implementing. Sustaining and consolidating. And whether the work is "secular" or "spiritual" matters little; there is much involved. Much is required. Much needs to be given. And sometimes we run on empty and do harm or even violence to the delicate membranes of our inner being.

A further contour may have to do with our frayed sense of calling. We never thought that the journey would be so long, the job so difficult, the career path so arduous, the spiritual ministry so taxing. Did we make good vocational choices? And if we did, how can we regroup and continue the journey? Most of us, therefore, know the cry for rest.

But rest is not enough. It is not simply a matter of some more hours of sleep. A deeper rest is called for—an inner rest. We need the rest of God's grace and acceptance. We need the rest of surrender where we hand to God our fears and worries and the things we cannot control or change.

We need the rest of being forgiven and forgiving. We need the rest of embrace where we know ourselves to be safe and secure in the goodness of God, in the wideness of his mercy, and in the comfort of the Spirit.

Our cry for rest is often much more a cry for those words that can most basically shape us: Well done, my beloved daughter, my beloved son. And in the shape of the human communities of which we are a part we also need to hear such words from our companions on the journey.

Exposure
A sorrowful cry

TO CRY OUT EITHER INWARDLY OR VERBALLY is part of the human condition. Sometimes the cry comes involuntarily: Oh, how wonderful! Or, Oh, no, how could I have done that! Some cries are mingled with joy and pain, as in the birth of a child. But some cries are harrowing. And none is more so than the painful cry of exposure and confession.

It is most unfortunate that this is so harrowing for us. But this is because exposure flies in the face of our entire socialization, where human autonomy, self-sufficiency, lack of vision for the common good, and the irrelevancy of a Supreme Being, have made notions of confession long out of date.

Why talk about failures and weaknesses when self-assertion is what is called for? It is better to keep hidden the weaker parts of ourselves lest others take advantage of us, our culture tells us.

That this is a fundamentally faulty set of ideas is evidenced by the chronic depression people suffer in our contemporary world and the way in which counselors and psychologists have become the "secular priests" of modern society.

But more specifically, this is existentially faulty because no human being can carry the weight of failure, shame, and wrongdoing without being drawn into a spiral of further, aberrant behaviors.

While this sorrowful cry is difficult for all people, it may be particularly difficult for certain Christians, including clergy. For it is so often that they function in the world with the idea that they are right, that people should see only their goodness, and that healthy witness and ministry come from a position of strength.

While I believe that the sorrowful cry cannot be expressed anywhere and anyhow, but should be divulged appropriately, I do believe that true ministry can come only from vulnerability and humility. In other words, it can come only from those who know how to acknowledge their struggles and failures.

Many of Henri Nouwen's writings show that he was not afraid to do this. In one of his self-disclosures he tells how his upward mobility "has been so filled with desires to be better than others, so marked by rivalry and competition, so pervaded with compulsions and obsessions, and so spotted with moments of suspicion, jealousy, resentment, and revenge."[3] This is quite a confession. This is a sorrowful cry. And all of us need to utter such cries, whether in the stillness of our own hearts in God's presence or to God in the presence of another person.

This need not be a morbid introspection. Instead, it can be the fruit of a reflective posture where we are willing to face the shadows within us, and face the darker side of who we are.

While this darkness may be shameful to ourselves, it is already known to God who calls us into the grace of his forgiveness and into the embrace of his healing presence. All the saints of the church have experienced an unveiling, a stripping down, and an exposure leading to a cry for mercy. No cry can be more healing and more freeing.

Conflicted
The cry of the divided heart

In our contemporary culture we speak a lot about the importance of being focused and single-minded. This is particularly the mantra of certain persons in the business world who have formulas for success and riches. This language is also sports-speak. One can become a successful athlete or swimmer or soccer player only by being totally focused on one's sport.

While this language is understandable, it is not the whole story. One may be focused on a particular activity, but life has a wider set of challenges and responsibilities. One may be a businessperson, but also a wife, mother, member of a number of nonprofit or civic groups, and part-time caregiver for one's aging father.

We cannot live only the one thing. And within a Christian framework this is unacceptable, since the biblical vision of life pulls us simultaneously in various directions: Love of God and love of neighbor. Caring for one's family, but also for the stranger and the poor. Commitment to the community of faith, but also to work in the world as a witness, reconciler, and healer. In one sense we can say that the way of God is anti-focus. Instead, it is an invitation to enter the wideness of God's love for the complexity of our world.

If all of this is not challenging enough, the picture becomes even more complicated in that we human beings are fundamentally conflicted. Not only are there the external beckonings, which cause us to waver and become sidetracked, but there are also the internal conflicts. We want something. But we also want something else. And we quickly tire of the very thing we have striven to attain. One cannot live well unless one addresses the conflict inside each one of us.

Henri Nouwen speaks of his own inner conflict. "I want to love God, but also to make a career. I want to be a good Christian, but also have my successes as a teacher, preacher, and a speaker. I want to be a saint, but also enjoy the sensations of the sinner. I want to be close to Christ, but also [be] popular and liked by many people."[4]

While one may quibble about some of the contrasts that Nouwen makes, the point is nevertheless clear. Internally we are often pulled in various directions. We want goodness to predominate, but evil is also part of our lives and world. We want to be generous, but we are often controlling and manipulative.

The cry of the divided heart is the cry of Christian spirituality. Paul, the apostle of Christ, uttered this cry in Romans, chapter seven: "I do not do what I want" (v. 15).

I also know the cry of the divided heart, particularly where I have been too cowardly to respond to the call of making a greater commitment in serving the poor in our world.

We all have moments of visionary clarity. We all have the tugs of heart that call us to greater self-giving and generosity. But we are fearful and pull back.

The cry of the divided heart is fundamental to the human condition. Virtue does not lie in our dividedness. But grace is present in the heart cry. For in that cry we desire to be different, and we look to God, that his way may be more fully sculpted in us so that it may adorn the shape of our inner house.

Aloneness
The cry for intimacy

MOST OF US, UNLESS WE ARE TERRIBLY ISOLATED, have a gaggle of people around us who are willing to give all sorts of advice and encouragement. Whether this advice comes from family or friends, we need to recognize that much advice comes from the perspective of the advice-giver. Advice does not always come with the interest of the recipient in view.

Often, advice misses the mark because the advice-giver has not lingered long enough to hear and to discern. Therefore, such advice needs to be resisted, and this often deepens the aloneness of the recipient.

When we say no to the well-meaning words of others, especially of family and friends, we experience a deepening disconnect. And we wonder whether our different perspective on things, our differing sensibilities, our different sense of direction and purpose, come from wisdom or arrogance.

My father gave me all sorts of good advice about a work trajectory. In the end, I chose a very different path, and this only deepened an already profound sense of being different and out of step with my family of origin. This scenario is but one gateway into a fundamental human reality, that of aloneness. And most of the advice we receive regarding this reality has to do with ways to escape it. But, I wish to turn that around and suggest that aloneness must be embraced if we are going to live with any healthy sense of individuation and participation in community.

The strange paradox that lies at the heart of this matter is that the avoidance of the embrace of aloneness makes our participation in relationships and in community difficult. You may have thought the opposite—that the rejection of aloneness fuels us for community. But this is not the case. Healthy community occurs when its participants know both the blessing of self-boundedness and the grace of active participation and sharing.

Aloneness is not a curse to be avoided but a grace to be embraced. Aloneness is the goodness of an inner centering that laces the pain of differentness, the challenge of making particular choices, the joy of going in another direction. Aloneness is an experience of the solitary nature of who I am at the core of my being.

It is this aloneness that one may open up to God. Henri Nouwen assures us that "Solitude is the way in which we grow into the realization that where we are most alone we are most loved by God. It is a quality of heart, an inner quality that helps us to accept our aloneness lovingly, as a gift from God."[5] Thus, our embrace of aloneness is at the same time the cry for intimacy. The deeper the one, the profounder the other. This embrace has nothing to do with an unhealthy self-preoccupation. It is simply recognizing one's uniqueness and differentness, sculpted and understood by God. And there is no greater grace than the blessing of acceptance in the face of one's differentness and aloneness.

God has little joy in seeing his creatures misform themselves into a gray uniformity. Instead, the God who made the world with kaleidoscopic beauty affirms us at the core of who we are and says: "I know you, do not be afraid." From the joy of this inner embrace can come the fruits of connectedness, friendship, solidarity, and community.

Expectations
The cry for more

THE WESTERN WORLD IS CHARACTERIZED by an insatiable desire for more. Productivity and profit, upward mobility, and increasing standards of living are keys to our social and economic existence.

This desire for things to be better, faster, more functional, and more available all has to do with enhancing our sense of self. We want things. We don't really need them.

The hunger for more has permeated our whole way of life. As a result, we live in the world as demanders. We are seldom grateful and celebrative. This sense of demand can also be drawn into our relationships and friendships. Henri Nouwen makes the observation that "We constantly feel tempted to want more from those around us than they can give. We relate to our neighbors with the hope . . . that they are able to fulfill most of our deepest needs, and then we find ourselves disillusioned, angry, and frustrated when they do not."[6]

That we need each other is a fundamental given of human existence. But to demand of others positions us in relationships of functionality and legalism. To demand is to coerce. It is a form of emotional violence.

And to insist that others give what they cannot is to risk bringing a deep schism into one's relationships. This occurs when we are so enamored with what we think we need, and so blind to the other person in terms of his or her gifts, time, resources, and abilities.

None of this is to suggest that we should not turn to others with our legitimate needs. Nor does it mean that we should not put demands on people who can do better in their work demands, home responsibilities, and schoolwork. What it does mean is that we cannot demand what others may not and cannot give. We cannot demand love or trust. We cannot demand forgiveness. We cannot demand careful attentiveness. These things can only be given freely. And we certainly cannot demand a love that the other person does not possess.

The life of demand is finally a dead-end street, for so often we end up at the wrong address. While we may think that a particular friend can meet our needs, this is frequently not the case. Others can do far less than what we expect.

The reason for this is that many of our needs, wants, and desires are cosmic and transcendental in nature. What I mean by that is that no human being can meet those needs anyway. Another person, for example, cannot give us personal significance. This is something we have to come to within ourselves. We have to learn to embrace who we are and what we do well and what we cannot do.

Healthy relationships are those where we journey with others, encourage and support them, and are supported in return. This has to do with mutuality. This is the opposite of a relationship of demand.

The cry for more is a belittlement of what we must be and do and undermines the grace and providence of God in our lives. The cry for more often needs to be converted or transmuted. Instead it needs to become the joy of appreciation for what is given and received.

A Fading Vision
The cry for renewal and recovery

WHILE MUCH OF LIFE IS ROUTINE AND REPETITIVE, and we all live certain rhythms of personal existence, there are moments for all of us where we see things with a luminosity that arrests our attention and may even turn us around.

We all have had moments of insight: A surprising inspiration, a picture of what can be. And this, at least momentarily, has lifted us onto another plane of existence.

This is particularly powerful when we catch a glimpse of what we can actually do, or make, or create when previously we thought that this was impossible. It's as if all the barriers are broken down. As if possibility takes on the hue of actuality.

This also happens within religious experience. People have significant and revelatory dreams. People have visions of God or angels. People have prophetic insight regarding what the church or society can be if there is repentance, healing, and transformation.

We all know something of this movement of the mystical and the transcendental in our lives. And while for some this may be more profound than for others, we all have heard whispers from the edge of eternity.

It is possible, however, to pay no attention to any of this. And conversely it is also possible to pay *too* much attention to this without prayerful and careful discernment, and as a result get caught up in an unhealthy subjectivism.

But to pay attention to these moments is a way for the Spirit of God to pull us forward. It is a way to remind us of God's desire to love, communicate, and guide us. It is a way by which we can move beyond the routines of daily existence.

It is also likely that these visions and dreams and nudges of the Spirit are easily forgotten. Henri Nouwen reminds us that "the taste of God's unconditional love quickly disappears when the addictive powers of everyday existence make their presence felt again."[7]

To say that somewhat differently: We are far more shaped by the values and ideas of our society than we realize. We more readily conform to the routine and familiar and quickly disregard the voices that come from the house of God's love.

As a result, the cry for renewal should ever characterize us. The prayer for God's Kingdom to be more fully revealed and for the Holy Spirit to enlighten us, is a prayer and cry that needs to be deeply embedded within our very being.

Rather than the cry for security, we need to hear more of the cry for revelation. This cry is necessary simply because we are safer in the ambit of God's way with us than in being encumbered in the way of the world. The light, love, and hope that the Spirit brings are a fuller way of living life than the tired consumerist clichés of our modern world.

The cry for renewal is the cry of a seeking heart that knows the voice of heaven.

Without Hope
The cry of doubt

WHILE WE MAY BEGIN THE JOURNEY OF LIFE with a gentle idealism, it is usually not too long before the sobering, and even wounding, experiences begin to sculpt a different perspective of life for us. Part of growing up is becoming "bloodied" in the process.

For many this sobering process is helpful and healthy. One cannot live well cocooned in naiveté. Hence the bruising experiences of life bring strength. And our woundedness may become a gateway for faith leading to homecoming and healing.

But this picture may not be a good indication of what happens to others. The difficulties of life can bring in their wake questions of doubt and the experience of hopelessness. For some, these become religious questions that throw serious doubt on God's sovereignty and goodness in the face of personal tragedy and the ongoing madness of violence and war in our world. For others, the questions of doubt are shafted home: It must be my fault, my life is jinxed. And this so often leads to self-doubt and self-pity. There are people who live with the general dread that their life is somehow "cursed."

But possibly for most, the experience of both the goodness as well as the difficulties of life lead to the building of walls around us. And that wall may have deep fortifications within what was once a tender heart and soul. Here the way of the heart has become constricted. Defensiveness and hardness begin to dominate the inner soulscape.

We have all met hard and ruthless people, people seemingly without conscience and without the milk of human kindness. It is easy to see this in others. It is much harder to see it within ourselves, especially when this hardness spreads like a slow-growing cancer within the fabric of our being.

So, while many of us may not completely shut the gate, most of us do close down certain parts of our inner house. Henri Nouwen puts it as follows: "[Y]ou hold fast to what is familiar, even if you aren't proud of it. You find yourself saying: 'That's just how it is with me. I would like to be different, but it can't be now. That's just the way it is.'"[8]

The icy fingers of doubt and resignation have gripped the human heart. And so one lives without openness regarding a future for these matters. One has shut down.

To have doubt is one thing, but to be without hope is another. To have shut the door is a further step, but cracks can appear in solid walls. Then sometimes trees spring up in the most barren and rocky terrain.

The beginnings of a turnaround usually do not start with some magic solution but with the cry of doubt. To pray a prayer of hopelessness is the beginning of prayer. And to start with acknowledging one's hardness is the beginning of hope.

The problem in the life of faith and prayer is not so much *what* we cry out to the heavens but that we don't cry out at all. The cry, whatever it may be, is an expression of life, while a sullen silence the rigor of death.

Brokenness
The cry of lament

WE ALL KNOW SOMETHING ABOUT THE BROKENNESS OF OUR LIVES, our families, and the institutions in which we participate. We all have experienced a lack of goodness from others. We can acknowledge the frailty of goodness in our own lives, and we too have hurt other people.

Sadly, dysfunctionalities are not only personal, they are also institutional. Many of us have participated in workplaces where managers were less than helpful and employment practices slightly crazy. My own early working life in the printing and publishing industry was under a boss who was a "panic merchant" and had no skills in managing the tyranny of the urgent.

But the brokenness of the world is even more general and global. There is an overwhelming sense that our world is deeply scarred by political, racial, and economic injustice.

Henri Nouwen expresses this lament. "I see millions of lonely, starving faces all over the world, and large piles of the dead bodies of people killed in cruel wars and ethnic conflict. Whose cup is this? It is our cup, the cup of human suffering. For each of us our sorrows are deeply personal. For all of us our sorrows, too, are universal."[9]

One may rightly ask: What can I do with all of this? How much crying is possible?

It seems to me that we ever face the risk of shutting down on the larger dimensions of life. So we constantly hear: I can barely cope with my personal, family, and work-related issues. I have no emotional space for global realities. And moreover, what can I really do about these things, anyway?

Thus, we primarily engage those issues that directly affect us. The sorrowful cry is primarily a personal cry about our needs and concerns.

And while all of this is appropriate and understandable, it is not the whole picture. More to the point, it does not reflect the major contours of the biblical story. In that story we hear of a God who cries for his people and his world. A God who longs to bring *shalom* to all of his creation, who cries out in pain for his wayward people who fail to be a light to the nations.

The biblical story centers on Christ, who takes the pain and sorrows of the whole world into his heart. We who become the followers of Christ are invited to enter into his suffering. We too become the sorrow bearers.

Our sorrowful cry must also be a cry on behalf of others, the millions who live lives of degradation. That cry must be both lament and prophecy. We cry to God for mercy. And we speak to the power-brokers of our world for justice.

But we can never just cry. We must also act. Prayer always leads to entering the fray. The movement of prayer is from God to neighbor.

This does not mean that we move from sorrowful prayer to triumphant praxis. Much of our work in serving the poor is marked by small steps forward in the midst of tears. Anyone who has worked at the grassroots level knows that there are no quick solutions, only painful, small steps in the right direction. Thus our very doing is a sorrowful crying that God will bless the meager work of our hands.

Forgiveness
A cry for mercy

THERE ARE MANY DIMENSIONS AND COLORS to the story of forgiveness. From the simplicity of a child saying sorry for having taken something within the parental home without asking, to a nation seeking forgiveness and making reparation regarding its colonization of its indigenous peoples, forgiveness is and remains one of the powerful forces in human interaction.

Seeking forgiveness for the wrongs we have done and extending forgiveness to those who have hurt us are among the most basic sacramental duties of the human community. And these are sacraments, for in the act of forgiveness there is grace and healing. Being forgiven is like being bathed with holy oil.

It should not surprise, however, that distortions can readily occur in relation to these sacraments. In some instances this grace has been removed from the general community and placed solely in the hands of priests. In other cases people have turned forgiveness into a dull submission to the perpetrators of abuse. In many cases forgiveness has been reduced to saying sorry without any intent to change one's behavior.

In this and other instances the very life that forgiveness offers has been emasculated, and it has become like stale bread rather than the bread of life.

The dynamics of life are missing in the gentle art of forgiveness when due to our own hardness of heart we will not forgive others, and due to our own insecurities we cannot receive the forgiving goodness that others seek to extend to us.

Henri Nouwen struggled with many insecurities. He saw himself as a deeply wounded man. As a result, he often felt himself unable or unworthy to receive the grace of forgiveness. He writes, "One of the great challenges of the spiritual life is to receive God's forgiveness. There is something in us humans that keeps us clinging to our sins and prevents us from letting God . . . do all the healing, restoring and renewing."[10]

Here lies the mystery of the power of forgiveness. To be forgiven is not so much to have one's slate wiped clean. It is not so much to move from the debit to the credit side of the ledger. Rather, to be forgiven is an invitation to live in a fundamentally different way with the one who has extended forgiveness. To be forgiven means that one can no longer live in the same way.

To receive God's forgiveness is to allow God to bathe you. Forgiveness is the politics of embrace. And in this embrace all our striving, resisting, rebelling, and reacting comes under the renewing breath of the Holy Spirit.

It is the depth and radicalness of this grace that both entices us and scares us. We are always, in some way, scared of God's renewing work. An embrace that changes us means that we are no longer in control, and we cannot see what long-term consequences that may have for us.

So often we need to cry for mercy, that God will give us the grace not to resist God's good, gentle, yet transformative way with us. Forgiveness is, therefore, not simply the assurance that God will no longer hold something against us. It is, instead, a step in the journey to a new way of life, a step that leads us to extend goodness to others and become healers and peacemakers in our world.

HEART TRANSFORMATIONS

The Joy and Challenge of Conversion and Renewal

As INHABITANTS OF THE TWENTY-FIRST CENTURY we are all too aware of the way in which our world continues to change. This is not only in the area of technology and workplace practices with its increasing demands, but also in the wider scheme of politics and economics. The Soviet Union, that old superpower, collapsed more than a decade ago, and the emerging powers of China and India wait in the wings while the United States enjoys its time in what will be a temporary limelight.

The face of Christianity has also radically changed. From being predominantly Western in the nineteenth century, contemporary Christianity has now become a majority world phenomenon. Over seventy percent of all Christians now live in the non-Western world, and new forms of church, worship, theology, and service have sprung into being, adding kaleidoscopic color and diversity to global Christianity.

While all sorts of changes are clearly discernible on the large screen of world history, as individuals, families, and small communities, we are not so sure what power lies in our hands to bring about change. In fact, we often feel quite powerless. In a world of much larger configurations of power, we doubt our own ability to be effective change agents.

But the malaise lies much deeper. We are also struggling with how much personal change is possible. Can I become more fully human? Can I be a much better person? And spiritually, can I become more fully transformed into Christ-likeness?

These more personal questions have become all the more pressing with the collapse of the older structures of Christendom and the ongoing marginalization of the church in the Western world. In many ways, Western Christianity is in transition, and this hardly puts it in a good place to provide certainty, security, and guidance. Many Christians feel that the church has lost its way, and at best they are but spiritual pilgrims and refugees.

It, therefore, comes as no surprise that many Christians are wrestling with what it means to be part of the life of the church, and more specifically what it means to a person of faith, prayer, and spirituality. Henri Nouwen also grappled with these matters. What is faith? What is prayer? What is the nature of contemplation? What does life in Christ look like? What of the work of the Holy Spirit? What about ongoing conversion? And what of God's work of renewal and transformation?

Heart transformations lie at the heart of Nouwen's vision of the Christian life. But none of this was a smooth road for Nouwen. Nor is it a smooth road for us.

Personal transformation is an invitation to faith and struggle. We see this struggle clearly in Nouwen's *The Road to Daybreak*, where he charts his journey from academia to his participation in the L'Arche communities. Ongoing conversion leading to an ever-greater conformity to the way of Christ is no tranquil road.

In *Beyond the Mirror*, in which Nouwen speaks about a clearer vision of the purpose of the Christian life and of heavenly realities, we see him struggling with maintaining that vision in the ensuing months and years. So easily the transformation of the heart becomes encased in the regularity of everyday life. He writes, "When I awoke from my operation and realized that I was not yet in God's house but still alive in the world, I had an immediate perception of being sent: sent to make the all embracing love of the Father known to people who hunger and thirst for love." But later he admits, "The taste of God's unconditional love quickly disappears when the addictive powers of everyday existence make their presence felt again."[11]

We do tire in the journey of faith. We do lose our way. But we can experience renewal and find new energies.

What all of this suggests is that there are no straight lines. There are seasons in the Christian life. There are times of inspiration. There are also times of repetition and continuity. But there are also radical turning points where faith is renewed and the hovering Spirit comes with power.

Heart transformation is the refreshing and renewing of God's gracious activity in our lives, and as such needs to be anticipated and received with joy.

Habitation
God's transformational presence

THE BEGINNINGS OF SPIRITUAL INNER TRANSFORMATION are wrapped in mystery. We will never be able to unwrap the dynamics of the beginnings of the seeking and longing heart and the way in which God moves toward us in the embrace of love.

But that an awakening occurs, that a meeting takes place, that faith buds, that an awareness of God's presence begins to permeate one's being, there can be no doubt.

I can still remember with immediate clarity the power and significance of the realization that receiving Christ meant that he was making his home with me. The beginnings of inner change are the beginnings of presence, God with us.

Henri Nouwen speaks much the same language, but places it in the unfolding of the story of salvation in the scriptural drama. He writes, "At first God was the God *for* us, our protector and shield. Then, when Jesus sent his Spirit, God was revealed to us as the God *within* us, our very breath and heartbeat."[12]

The beginnings of inner transformation may well lie beyond our initial willing and doing. God is gently and mysteriously at work in people's lives well before they become aware of the birthing that may soon take place. But inner renewal does call forth our response. And the beginning of that response is usually a gnawing sense of need.

This sense of need varies. For some, the search for God comes from a profound sense of aloneness. For others, the search for significance and purpose finds its starting point in the embrace of living God's way in the world. For others, a sense of guilt and shame drives them to look for God's redemptive presence. And for others again, a sense of powerlessness drives them to seek the God who liberates and empowers his people.

It does not matter what is the conscious need, for our needs are always greater than our awareness of them. What matters is that the seeking heart and the seeking God meet.

There are no limitations as to how and where this meeting may occur. For some this may be a gentle unfolding and awakening. For others this meeting may be a dramatic encounter, where one experiences a radical reorientation. And in all the settings of life, not simply the sanctuary, God is a God who seeks us out.

This meeting is neither a chance meeting nor a temporary encounter. God does not come simply to say hello. God comes to stay.

The beginnings of a spiritual inner transformation have to do with habitation. God in Christ through the Holy Spirit invites us to make our home with the Trinity. And the Father, Son, and Holy Spirit make their home within our being.

Inner transformation requires a long journey of faithful companionship and care. And that is what God offers us, a covenant faithfulness that is strong enough to cope with our changing sensibilities.

While some would like the inner transformation to be complete in one act of conversion, change does not come that easily. The movement of change is not simply *from* something that is undesirable. It more particularly is a change *to* something that is desirable. And that is conformity to God's ways. For this only the long journey will do.

Solitude
The place of transformation

COMING TO FAITH IN THE GOD OF ALL GOODNESS AND GRACE is the beginning of a long journey of growth and transformation. There are many contours on this road. There are setbacks and doubts as well. But there are also the points of renewal and hope.

One of the elements in the moment or season of renewal is the practice of the discipline of solitude. At its most basic level this is a growing awareness of the need to be still and to become attentive to the voice of God and movement of the Spirit within us.

This is the opposite of how we most frequently function. We are active. We are busy. We know what we should do, and so we live life in full stride. We pray that God will bless all our endeavors.

But there are times when this all becomes very uncertain. We are no longer sure that what we are doing is worthwhile. We are no longer sure that God is blessing us.

Since newfound hope and purpose can't simply be grasped out of thin air, the only way forward in times of doubt and uncertainty is to stop and to wait. This can become the starting point for entering into a season of the careful practice of solitude.

While the practice of solitude should be part of the normal rhythm of our lives, it becomes particularly important and pressing in times of difficulty and need. Entering into solitude is making a break with our more normal existence. It comes from a recognition that not all is well, and we need to find new bread for the journey of faith.

Moving from activity to stillness and from stillness to solitude is a move toward a new attentiveness to God and a new openness to God's Spirit. The outcome of this new attentiveness, while it may be to affirm the familiar, is often transformational. God encounters us and speaks to us in ways we had not anticipated.

Henri Nouwen suggests that "solitude is the furnace of transformation. Without solitude we remain victims of our society and continue to be entangled in the illusions of the false self."[13]

The reason that the practice of solitude can be so transformational is that solitude distances us from our own activities and preoccupations and brings us close to the seeking and renewing heart of God. The God who speaks in the silence of our hearts is the God who seeks to make us whole and to guide us in the paths of righteousness.

God draws near to those who seek, wait, and pray. And God's closeness is always one of embrace and empowerment. In that embrace we may see ourselves and the world very differently. As the beloved of God we may find that our insecurities fall away. And as those guided in the ways of God we may see our life's circumstances and our world in the light of God's presence.

Solitude is the framework for the gift of contemplation, and a radical reorientation is so frequently the gift that God gives. No longer do the old ways define and shape us, but God's gracious presence opens the way for newfound hope, love, and direction.

Transformation is not the gift of those who grasp but the blessing of those who wait for God to move the waters.

In the Spirit
In touch with the Great Transformer

IT IS EVER SO EASY to gain the impression that living the Christian life has everything to do with *our* faithfulness, commitment, and prayer. This spills over into self-effort. The Christian life is then what we make of it.

That this is both half the story and a skewing of the story is evidenced by the fact that the Bible gives us a very different picture. In its pages we hear an alternative to the drumbeat of self-effort.

The biblical story speaks of the God who seeks us out. The God who in mercy desires our wholeness. The God who reaches into the dark places of our hearts and pours healing oil on our inner woundedness.

But there is more to this amazing story.

Its central heartbeat is that God pours out the Spirit into our lives and that we live the life of faith renewed, sustained, and empowered by the Spirit. The breath of the Spirit blows us onto the paths of God's way for us.

Thus living the Christian life is not first of all what *we* do. It is what God has done *for us* through the grace of Christ, and what God does *in us* through the presence of the Holy Spirit.

Christian spirituality is not simply living in conformity with Christian doctrines and its ethical ideals. It is not simply being part of the Christian church. Christian spirituality is not simply a way of life in harmony with the gospel. Christian spirituality has a much deeper inner wellspring.

That wellspring is none other than that one has been impacted by the presence of the living God. And this is work of the Holy Spirit.

Henri Nouwen expresses this as follows: "The spiritual life is that life of those who are reborn from above—who have received the Spirit of God who comes to us from God. That life allows us to break out of our prison of human entanglements and sets us free for a life in God."[14]

The Spirit is also the great heart surgeon. Knowing the intimate places of the human heart, both its visionary goodness and its demonic misformations, the Spirit as the careful scalpel bearer brings healing and well-being to one's inner self. The ultimate work of the Spirit is to renew all the broken places in the inner sanctum of our lives.

The Spirit is also the great artistic renovator. The reshaping of our values and our desires is the key work of the Spirit. And this reshaping is bringing us into conformity and harmony with the way of Christ. The God-honoring, forgiving, healing, peacemaking, and community-building way of Christ, the concern for the poor as important to the way of Christ, is slowly, but surely, forged into our inner being through the work of the Holy Spirit.

Ever present. Ever so subtle. Ever so self-effacing. Ever so purging and rescuing. Ever so healing and transforming. Ever so enriching and empowering, is the presence of the Holy Spirit.

Heart transformation is the specialty of the Spirit. We are invited to receive the Spirit, live in the Spirit, embrace the gifts of the Spirit, and be sustained and blown along by the very breath of God.

Compulsions
Transforming our inner motivations

THE JOURNEY OF TRANSFORMATION into the image and likeness of Christ is never a call for change that has to do only with spiritual activities such as prayer and meditation. The transformation that Scripture has in view is a full-orbed one. It is a transformation that has all of a person in view: the personal and the social, the inward and the outward, the spiritual and the political.

Some do not see this integral perspective. They hold that the following of Christ has primarily to do with the afterlife. Others see their relationship with Christ primarily in terms of developing inner virtues. Others again see Christian discipleship within the frame of the work for peace and justice.

But growth in Christ and walking in the way of Christ involves all of this and more. No human activity is excluded from God's concern. No part of our lives is out of bounds for the renewing and transforming work of the Spirit, including our genetic and social shaping and configuration.

While one may speak about a certain predisposition in terms of who we are physically, emotionally, intellectually, there is no suggestion that the human being is simply predetermined and programmed. Change and growth are possible. And the gracious renewing work of God in our lives can bring about a shift in our motivations and orientation.

This is not to suggest that this happens overnight or comes prepackaged with our conversion. It is a process. God's healing grace is for all the areas of our lives where we have become wounded and things have become skewed and even twisted.

Henri Nouwen confesses: "I know too well how hard it is to live without being needed, being wanted, being asked, being known, being admired, being praised."[15] And I can add: I know how easy it is for me to be functional rather than relational, overdoing things rather than balancing activity with Sabbath, activity-centered rather than prayerful, self-protective rather than vulnerable.

So there are things in us that need to change. Conversion and coming to faith are not the end but merely the beginning of this transformational process. And these called-for changes in our way of thinking and doing won't come easily as scattered seed from the sower's hand.

The changes that will reorient our inner compulsions that spring so often from our wounded self, come by way of purgation and painful transformations. Inner change involves self-confrontation, disarmament, relinquishment, and the journey toward wholeness. On this road there are no shortcuts and certainly no quick fixes.

God's renewing work is not to do violence to us but to heal us and make us whole. This is the strong but gentle work of God. This is purging the darkness and healing the wounded places.

None of us can escape this sculpting of God's Spirit within our lives. We may long be oblivious to our own needs. We may long resist the gracious healing hand of God. But finally we do need to yield ourselves into the hands of the One who made all things and seeks to make us whole.

Relational Healing
Transforming our relationships

SINCE THE INNER AND THE OUTER DIMENSIONS OF LIFE are intimately interrelated, I am not so sure whether it is possible for a person to be inwardly pious and socially dysfunctional. Inner transformations have outward implications. A love within is soon evidenced by a love for others, including the stranger and possibly even the enemy.

Heart transformations cannot remain matters of the heart. These changes ought to run over the spillway and make fruitful a barren land.

The spillover of the transformations of the heart is a way of being profoundly countercultural. Our Western way of life so much has the individual primarily in view. Much of this way of life has to do with my needs and my happiness. And my self-development tends to be the primary focus.

This emphasis has also invaded much of the contemporary Western church. So often, our churches are characterized by a consumer mentality, and spirituality is primarily cast in personal terms. Many of our churches know little of the praxis of community. Or in the words of Henri Nouwen, "not solidarity but fragmentation is the most visible quality of the way people relate to each other." He goes on to remind us that "God wants to open our eyes so that we can see that we belong together in the embrace of God's perfect love."[16]

Therefore, the theme of relational healing is an appropriate topic for us to consider. Can the changes within us, due to the grace of Christ and the working of the Holy Spirit, bring about such inner transformations that community becomes a song we want to sing and a story we want to live?

This kind of transformation is possible. It has happened before. We see it in the dangerous memories of Early Christianity such as we read about in the Acts 2–4 story. We see it in the long history of monasticism. We see it in the early Anabaptists, in the Moravians, in the Wesleyan Movement, and in the Basic Christian Communities in Latin America and the house churches of the First World.

Not only is it possible and has it been done before, but also the very nature of the Christian faith calls for such a transformation. Being transformed by Christ includes a transformation in our relationships. The renewal of the Spirit draws us into a love for our brothers and sisters in the faith and the love of neighbor.

This love, at the heart of community building, is not mere sentimentality. It is a love that walks the long road of commitment, solidarity, and service. Being in Christ through the Spirit, and therefore part of the community of faith, involves us in more than worship, teaching, and sacrament. It involves us in more than only praying for one another. It also calls us to the journey of encouragement, mutual care, and economic sharing.

The transformations of the heart require not only growth in the love of God and in the disciplines of the spiritual life. They also require growth in love and care for those within whose faces we are to see the face of Christ, including the hidden and disfigured sense of his presence.

A Renewed Listening
Transforming those inner voices

IT IS BOTH INTERESTING AND NECESSARY for us to reflect on our own inner talking. Most of us talk a lot to ourselves. And much of what we have to say is not necessarily good or helpful. Much of our self-talk is negative. For some, their inner world is the ever-running broken record of insecurity, woundedness, and fear.

I know something of this inner world. The formative years of my life without the presence of my father because of war and immigration, left me insecure, reactive, and aggressive. Mine was a confused inner world.

Those who have read many of the writings of my conversation partner in these reflections will know that Nouwen long suffered from insecurities, a sense of rejection, and from an uncomfortability regarding his own personhood. This led either to a crowded clinging to or a sense of rage toward others.

What we need to recognize is that our self-talk is never simply our own talk, for these inner voices are also the voices of others and the wounding we have received at their hands. It is also possible that our inner voice picks up the vibrations of generational dys-functionalities. In extreme cases our inner voices may become the voice of a split personality or the voice of demonic forces.

We can't ignore these inner voices. While the extreme cases need careful pastoral and professional attention, the transformation of our inner voices is essential to our inner healing and general well-being. The journey of faith can't ignore being attentive to the confusion and sometimes chaos within.

The starting point in what may be a long process of inner renewal is the gift and ability to hear another voice. A contrary voice. A voice of a very different melody.

It is usually not the case that this voice is so loud that it drowns out our own inner voices. Rather, it is that this voice is so winsome that it begins to subvert and destabilize our inner voices. Nouwen speaks of the necessity "to be empty, free, and open, conscious of God-with-us, sensing God present, listening with our hearts to the voice of love."[17] This voice is none other than the whispers of the Spirit, the very breath of the God of love.

To hear in the very depths of my being that God has known me from the very beginning, even while I was being formed in my mother's womb; to hear that in Christ God's love is for me and toward me; to hear that God sees me and loves me with unbounded grace; to hear that I may shelter in his presence and be fed at his banqueting table—to hear these voices brings hope to the most insecure, fearful, angry, and broken parts of our lives.

This voice of love echoes in the heart chambers of the whole of humanity. Its whispers are also in our own hearts. We need a new attentiveness to hear it, for sadly we seem to prefer the familiar voices of chaos than the Voice that can set us free.

While we may wish that God would shout, the Voice of love can already be heard. It echoes from a rugged cross. Its richly textured melodies lie secure within the Gospel stories. And the pervasive voice of the brooding Spirit seeks to awaken us to the Voice that can dynamite or erode our inner voices of fear, distrust, and anxiety.

Downward Mobility
Transforming our goals and values

M<small>OST MATURE PEOPLE</small> seek to engage in careers that bring about self-enhancement and self-development, enabling one to enjoy status and position, and ensuring economic security and well-being. At the same time, these people will seek to make some contribution to the overall good in society.

These same people recognize that there is also a dark side to the workplace. We may have chosen the wrong career. We may lose our jobs. The good that we sought to achieve may have unintended consequences. And we may lose our way in our career and suffer from ill health and despair.

Notwithstanding the difficulties, our culture lauds the major contours of the possible dimensions of the above scenario. It is pragmatic. It is responsible. And it is self-serving, with an appropriate nod to general social responsibility.

That many Christians have also bought into this picture should not surprise us. Our all-pervasive culture, which celebrates the values of contemporary capitalism, has successfully spread its gospel of untrammeled progress, productivity, and prosperity. In the church it has also found a home.

That the biblical story seeks to throw some shadows over this grand scenario, and probes this ethic with disturbing questions, may be a surprise to some. But that is precisely what the Bible does, this book of great hope and of disturbing ideas.

With the central idea that God (and not the human being) is the pivotal point of life, that the way of Christ and not our way is to be our way in the world, and that worship, obedience, and service are to form and shape our involvement in the world, it can readily be seen that the world's way of orchestrating the symphony of life needs a different score.

The Christian is called to live a world-affirming way of life. This means participating in all the affairs of life and making a contribution. But the Christian has also heard another voice and knows a different melody.

This music has to do with living Christianly in our world. And this is following Christ in the midst of daily life. It is emulating the way of Christ. It is being Christ-like. And it is seeking to be a witness to Christ whether one is a police officer, a businessperson, a priest, an artist, or a house-painter.

One of the dimensions of living the way of Christ, besides living a life of love, forgiveness, and service, is embracing the spirituality of downward mobility. This is a willingness to modify our career, change our location, or whatever other sacrifices we are called to make, for the sake of following Christ in the service of others.

Henri Nouwen reminds us that Christ himself practiced downward mobility. In "Jesus Christ," he reminds us, "is the displaced Lord in whom God's compassion becomes flesh. In him we see a life of displacement lived to the fullest."[18]

The follower of Christ can hardly expect to walk a different road. For the sake of Christ, who is to be central and Lord, other things, including our career and our security, will have to take second place. And we will have to live our career and our security in a different way.

Thus the calling of Christ, the values of God's reign, the ethos of the gospel will modify the way we make life choices, the job we do, the priorities we set, and the values we hold.

Heart transformations through Word and Spirit will so revolutionize us that both the way we work, where we work, and the kind of work we are called to do will demonstrate that the grace of Christ as inward reality becomes part of the public domain.

Growing Up
Transforming a Sunday school faith

A CHILD'S WORLD, if it is in any way imaginative, is readily filled with trust, with belief, with magic. The impossible is possible. Dreams come true. The good prevails. And the God in heaven makes everything right and good.

By adolescence many of these and other hopeful ideals lie shattered like shards of pottery on a concrete floor. Life has a way of bloodying us. We soon discover that things are not that simple.

We also soon discover that the life of faith is not quite what we had thought or expected. God did not help us win the baseball game, did not prevent our mother dying from cancer. And the church with its liturgy and stained glass windows, its stories of faith, and the praxis of its life together, soon turns out to be something less than what we had hoped for.

All of this is to be expected. And it is a phase in the journey of life we have to negotiate.

Henri Nouwen in one of his earlier writings speaks of the fact that "healthy development means a gradual movement out of the magical world."[19] By this he does not mean that we deny faith and embrace rationality. What he means is that we have to grow beyond the idea of God as a comfort blanket. In other words, we have to grow beyond a Sunday school faith.

Some people do not negotiate these waters very well, with their tricky currents. They abandon the journey of faith. If God does not, or will not, or cannot do what I reasonably ask, particularly when it comes to sickness and tragedy in our family and world, then this is not the God I wish to associate with!

The transformations that are called for if we are to move to a more mature faith are by no means easy. There is nothing easy about learning to love and follow the God who does not protect us from all of life's difficulties and ills. Neither is it easy to journey with the God who abandoned his own Son to a cruel death. Nor is it easy to believe in a God who watched over his followers as they were being thrown to the lions.

It is certainly a challenge to have faith in a God who prefers mystery to magic and who is silent as much as he speaks. The journey toward a mature faith involves a willingness to embrace God for who he is rather than what we would like God to be. It is bowing before his sovereignty and mystery. And it involves a willingness to embrace the way of God in our world, which is not the way of grandiose power, but the way of vulnerable humility.

God's way is the way of love, not coercion. It is the way of faith, not rationality. It is the way of forgiveness, not demand. It is the way of freely given grace, not manipulative magic.

Just as there are phases in human development and in the formation of organizations and institutions, so there are the critical transition points in the journey of faith, in the life of discipleship. Heart transformations have to do not only with coming to faith but also with growing in faith. The one is as challenging as the other. Both call for conversion, courage, and abandonment into the brooding presence of the Spirit who seeks to guide us through troubles and difficult waters.

The transition from a Sunday school faith to a mature faith is not so much the move from childishness to adulthood. It is rather a move from following the God of our own making to following the God of the biblical story. This move does not make us smart and all-knowing about God. Rather, it calls us to greater faith, humility, and childlikeness.

The Vulnerable Ones
Strange agents of transformation

RENEWAL, TRANSFORMATION, AND HEALING can come to us in many ways and from many different sources. The body can heal itself. A secular university professor may, in fact, open a new thought and direction in our lives just as easily as a more "spiritual" source can.

While Christians believe that wholesome change can come through prayer, the sacraments, the hearing of the gospel, and the pastoral ministry of the church or their brothers and sisters in the faith, they also believe that blessings can and do come in many other ways. This is because they believe that God through the Spirit is wonderfully and mysteriously at work in the world. God works through the church but also in and through the world.

This makes the journey of faith a wonderfully open space. The Christian life has nothing to do with narrowing the arteries of one's inner being. Instead, the life of faith is opening one's heart to the God of surprises.

But this, of course, is more easily said than done. The surprises of God are often strange. And we may well be resistant to or completely miss seeing the good that comes our way. I remember, for instance, a work colleague who was stridently anti-religious. And yet, I realize now, he cared for me in many ways and challenged me regarding the way I was living my faith.

Nouwen has written about the way in which his care for Adam, a severely disabled person, became a ministry of receiving and not only one of giving. Nouwen writes, "[In] his weakness he [Adam] became a unique instrument of God's grace. He became a revelation of Christ among us." He continues, "I am not saying that Adam was a second Jesus. But I am saying that because of the vulnerability of Jesus we can see Adam's extremely vulnerable life as a life of utmost spiritual significance."[20]

That God uses unlikely people for his purposes is everywhere writ large in the biblical story: Moses the murderer. Amos a mere orchard worker. Mary an impoverished maiden. Simon the political radical and disciple of Christ.

While we may want the experience of God's unmediated presence—and those moments may be there, and we may want God's Spirit to bless us in the sanctuary—and that may well occur, God also has other ways to renew and transform us. To do the gracious work of inner rehabilitation that draws us into greater conformity to Christ and the wholeness that this brings, God, ever at work in us and in the world, uses unlikely candidates.

Seldom are the instruments of God's goodness the powerful of this world. More frequently God uses the vulnerable ones of the earth. But always God uses only the humble, those who wait on God and who know that their hope and strength is in God alone.

All of this poses a great challenge to the present ethos of many of our churches, where Christians still see themselves as powerful in resources and having much to give. As a consequence, dependency on God is not a characteristic posture. Ours is the challenge of receptivity. To enter more fully into the life that God seeks to give, we require an openness that will enable us to move slowly enough and to be close enough to the Adams of this world whom God may use to draw us into greater love and wholeness.

A Servant's Heart
Transformation through giving

THE MOVEMENT OF GOD'S GOODNESS in our lives results in neither our self-negation nor our self-enhancement, but in an inner transformation that seeks to spill out into every aspect of our lives.

The new emerging self in Christ, shaped by the gospel and sculpted by the Spirit, is a self that echoes the heartbeat of Christ. And embedded in this echo is a heart that seeks to serve.

Henri Nouwen has put this well as a double movement of the Christian life. This is the movement of transcendence and incarnation. This is a movement toward God and toward our neighbor. He writes, "as prayer leads us into the house of God and God's people, so action leads us back into the world to work there for reconciliation, unity, and peace."[21]

While receiving is foundational to our inner growth and transformation, giving is the fruit of that inner healing. But it is never only the fruit; it also contributes to our growth and well-being.

If this perspective is lacking, then service can so easily become difficult and dulling. Service so readily slips a gear or two. It becomes a demand, duty, and burden.

In our discipleship and the journey of faith, if we can avoid the shoals of self-negation that springs from an unhealthy asceticism, and avoid the craggy and slippery slopes of self-enhancement that echoes the narcissism of our time, then we may be able to grow into a way of being where service comes from a good place.

Such service is not a service to make us feel good. It is not service for the sake of some ideological cause, including a Christian cause. It is not service as a form of control or seeking to extend our influence. Instead, it is service for the sake of the other. It is service that seeks to bless and to extend God's *shalom* and goodness to the other person.

This kind of service is not servantile. It is not something that denigrates either the giver or the receiver. It is a service that makes the giver and receiver whole.

Service therefore is not us paying our dues. It is not a form of repayment. Service is not the tasks we are called to because God has blessed us and renewed us in Christ.

Seeking to serve and to be a blessing to others in whatever form that may take—witness, care, advocacy, prayer, giving, and the work of justice—comes from the love of God in us that recognizes the marks of God in the other person. This makes service worship. It makes it a sacrament.

Heart transformations may occur in the private place of prayer and solitude They may also occur in the sanctuary with its worship, word, sacrament, and fellowship. But God may also use the place of work or the goodness of our neighbor to draw us into greater wholeness. And the goodness we seek to extend to others may well return to us in unexpected ways. The full cup that we carefully hold for ourselves will run empty. The cup we give to others may well be the cup from which we are refreshed when we thought it was empty.

HEART
AND HEAD

The Journey and Empowerment of
Faith Seeking Understanding

IT HAS BECOME A BIT OF A CULTURAL CLICHÉ that people of faith are often regarded as incredulous and operate out of subjectivism and emotionalism. In more recent times that cliché has taken on a much darker hue because of the religious fanaticism so evident among various religious groups. Thus, faith has become for many onlookers not only subjective, but also irrational and dangerous.

While global humanity continues to be divided into various major religious camps, the growth in our time is with those who claim no religious affiliation whatsoever. Little wonder. Why throw away your mind, why embrace irrationality, and why become fanatical in order to celebrate some religious experience!

But does a faith commitment necessarily lead to incredulity? Does it involve irrationality? Does it lead to bigotry? It may and it does. But it need not and should not!

51

While faith can be drunk in a pristine stream, it may also be drunk in very muddied waters. Religious systems and institutions, while called to be the carriers of life-giving waters, may well have become rusty pipes and conduits. As a result, faith can be mixed with ideology. Or equally disconcerting but seemingly benign, faith can be shaped by major cultural forces that end up subverting faith.

Faith, therefore, needs to be thought about. This is not only in order to identify accretions that don't belong to faith; indeed, the very nature of faith is to seek understanding.

We want to understand the meaning and significance of a particular spiritual experience. We want to understand this within our faith tradition. We want to know how others in the past made sense of similar experiences.

Within the pages of the biblical story we see this movement. The Old Testament "I am that I am" is understood to be Yahweh, the liberating and covenant-making God of the Israelites. The Man from Galilee is seen to be the Christ as Lord of history.

We are invited in the pages of Scripture to love God with heart and mind. And as we live the life of faith we want to know God better and seek to understand more fully the ramifications of faith for all the contours of our life and our involvement in the world.

Henri Nouwen was the first to admit that he was no systematic theologian. He was a priest. He trained in psychology. He pursued further theological studies, but he primarily taught Christian spirituality. He was pre-eminently a pastor. And most fundamentally he was a person who bared his own soul. It is for this reason that his many readers have found his writings so accessible for their own struggles in the faith journey.

But Nouwen's writings do contain an articulated faith. There is substance to his understanding of living the Christian life. And we are invited to do the same. We, too, need a faith that engages the head as well as the heart.

Head and heart. Heart and head. These belong together. To say I believe in Jesus Christ must be followed by an articulation of who this Jesus is. Is he both Son of Man and Son of God? Is he both the son of Mary and the second person of the Trinity?

The articulation of faith places it in the public arena. Faith cannot be simply my personal preference. It belongs to public discourse. Christian faith has been thought about from the early Church Fathers through to Thomas Aquinas, later by the Reformers, and into our present time by both First World and Third World theologians. In this, reflective reader, may our heart inform our head. May our head sink deeply into our heart. And may we have a faith that is passionate and thoughtful, spiritual and reflective, contemplative and active.

Seeing
Where mystery and faith meet

THE CHRISTIAN FAITH EMBODIES A NUMBER OF CENTRAL BELIEFS. Among these are that the created order is God's handiwork. Humanity is made in God's image and therefore is called to live in relationship with God and in community with one another.

Further key beliefs are that human beings have a propensity to live in other ways than to the glory of God and to the blessing of others. We tend to be self-seeking and self-serving. And while capable of great good, we do much harm.

Our flight from God and our failure in relation to one another and to our mandate to care for God's world, places us in a position of needing help. God's help. A help that brings about our healing.

This help has been generously extended to humanity through the ages. The nature of this help has been most clearly displayed by the love of God in Christ to bring us home and make us whole.

The heartbeat of what all this is about is union with God. It is living more fully in the presence of God, who sustains us and who seeks to reorient our lives so that we live out of a new center and with a new vision. This new center is that we live in and for God rather than that we live out a social self shaped by the values of our own old world order. The new vision is that we seek to live out of the love of God in Christ in order to be the peacemakers and healers that our fragmented and war-torn world so urgently needs.

To live with and for God makes us the visionaries of a new world order not created by force or the sword or the bomb, but by God's peaceable Spirit. This makes us into contemplatives who in faith and prayer see the footprints of God's presence, the signs of the Reign of God, the movement of the Spirit even in the places of seeming hopelessness and despair.

Henri Nouwen once made the comment, "[T]he great mystery of the contemplative life is not that we see God in the world, but that God within us recognizes God in the world."[22] Put differently, the heart of the Christian experience is a new seeing: of ourselves, of others, and of the world in and through the love of God.

All of this can be understood and said in many ways, but the central theme is the same. The pulsating heartbeat is that my life is no longer woven around a wounded autonomous self but finds itself bathed and anointed in the healing love of God.

This gives us a new center, a new heart, a new way of seeing things, a new way of thinking about life and our world.

With these eyes of faith we can begin to pray and to think and to work for the healing and transformation of our neighborhoods, institutions, and world, while we ourselves need to be ever more fully drawn into this new life that God gives.

Beyond Dualism
Where faith and world meet

GOD IS NOT A SELF-EVIDENT GIVEN, particularly not in a world of hunger, earthquakes, tsunamis, and hurricanes, a world of Hitler, Stalin, and Pol Pot. Nor can one simply point to something and say "there is God." This cannot even be done by pointing to a cathedral, synagogue, mosque, or temple.

Within the Christian tradition God and church are not one and the same. Nor is God's reign synonymous with the community of faith. The church at best is a sign, servant, and sacrament of the Kingdom of God.

One of the first things one would have to say is that God is Wholly Other. We are but creatures sculpted by God's hands of love and care.

But in the same breath one may also say that this God has entered the human fray. In word and deed, in priest and prophet, and particularly in Christ, God has come among us. Wholly Other, God is yet also wholly concerned. Transcendent, yet incarnate, God the mysterious One is the God of self-disclosure and welcome.

But this also is not self-evident. The belief that God is with us and among us and that God is at work in our world is always a confession of faith. This confession can come only when by God's Spirit our hearts and minds have been opened to see and hear.

Henri Nouwen writes that the "contemplative life is a human response to the fundamental fact that the central things in life, although spiritually perceptible, remain invisible in large measure and can very easily be overlooked by the inattentive, busy, distracted person that each of us can so readily become."[23]

This need not be the language of an older dualism where heaven and earth, spiritual and material, soul and body were seen in oppositional terms, with the one being greater than the other. Rather, this may be the language that sees creation as God's good gift, the body as habitation for God's Spirit, and the world as charged with the grandeur of God.

This does not mean that the other world is wholly present in this one. If that were the case nature would be fully healed and the evils of humanity would be absorbed and transformed by God's purging love that makes all things new and whole.

The final tension lies neither between heaven and earth, nor between body and soul, nor between the spiritual and the material. It lies between faith and non-faith, between obedience to the ways of God and persistence in our own waywardness.

The tension is not between Spirit and world, it is the worldliness of the world at loggerheads with the gospel of the Kingdom of God, which speaks of forgiveness, healing, reconciliation and peacemaking, and wholeness.

Dancing this gospel into the world means that love not violence, prayer not coercion, forgiveness not retaliation, hospitality not exclusion, healing not harming become the footprints of our daily existence. Thus one may say God is among us. The other world is already present. But the old world persists.

But when we march to a tune that brings fear rather than hope, and death rather than life, then conversion is called for, repentance becomes necessary, and transformation is needed. For then we emulate the old world rather than being the heralds of the new world that God is calling into being.

Knowability and Mystery
Where curiosity and humility meet

MADE IN GOD'S IMAGE, humans have been gifted with untold capacities and abilities. Shaped by the good hand of the Creator God, human beings have the gift of creativity. The whole human enterprise of family, community, institution, and nation-building demonstrates the human capacity for responding to challenges and creating environments of sustenance, safety, care, and beauty. That there is also a dark side to this human enterprise is stating the obvious.

In this vast economic and cultural enterprise it is possible that humans see themselves at the center of all of this and "worship" the work of their own hands. Humans can forget or neglect the vision that they are sustained by God's caring grace and that thankfulness and humility should characterize their existence rather than a *hubris* that exalts human ingenuity.

It is self-evident that we know much about ourselves and our world. But there is also much that we do not know. It is appropriate that we may live in the quest of further discovery as well as in the humility of the mystery of the complexity of who we are and the grandness of our natural and social worlds.

This quest, sculpted by humility, is also a basic posture for the journey in the spiritual life. This is a journey of wonderment, reflection, prayer, and faith.

Henri Nouwen speaks of this posture: "Poverty of mind as a spiritual attitude is a growing willingness to recognize the incomprehensibility of the mystery of life. The more mature we become the more we will be able to give up our inclination to grasp, catch, and comprehend the fullness of life and the more we will be ready to let life enter us."[24]

All of this is not to default to the language of mystery at the limits of our knowability. Mystery lies at the heart and beyond our knowability. The more we know the more we are humbled. The greater our understanding the greater our sense of wonderment.

Wonderment may well be the midwife that brings forth the act of worship that lauds the Creator, celebrates the gift of life, and is awed by the goodness that comes our way despite the world's brokenness and pain.

To know is also to be known, and the most profound sense of recognition comes not simply from family and friends, but from the God who calls us beloved. Beloved despite our failures, insecurities, and sin.

We may know much about much, although usually we know much about very little. A self-knowing that is not fretful, fearful, and self-recriminating, but is bathed in the generous love of the Great Other who calls me by name and welcomes me, is a knowing that centers all our other knowing. Bathed in the waters of grace and forgiveness and gently held in the hands of the Architect and Maker of all, I may pursue the quest for knowledge not simply to assuage my own pain but to live in a wonder that sees all made well in God's beneficence.

Explanations That Don't Explain
Where apologetics and witness meet

ANYONE WHO HAS BEEN IMPACTED BY THE GRACE and goodness of God in Christ and who begins to live in and out of that reality, will quickly begin to wonder how others may also share and participate in the generosity of such goodness. We, therefore, should never be surprised at the fundamental impulse for mission, which lies at the heart of the convert.

Just as beggars finding bread will share a morsel with others, and concentration camp escapees will want to include other prisoners in the dash for freedom, so the discoverers of the love of God, the freedom in Christ, and the gift of the Spirit, will want others to enjoy the same blessings.

That converts want to do this is understandable. That they always do this well is open to question.

From the early Church Fathers as apologists right up to the present, various strategies have been used by members of the community of faith to explain the Christian faith to others. The best motivation has been to share the love of God with others. That Christians have been motivated in other ways is a sad part of the story of Christian witness.

Unfortunately, explanations did not always explain. The early Church Fathers claimed that the best of Greek wisdom had the wisdom of Christ implicitly embedded within it. And the apologists of later Christendom, with its collusion with modernity, attempted to explain God in rational ways. And the missionary effort during the colonial period was premised on sharing the superior Western God along with a supposed superior Western culture.

So is it a matter of explanation or of sharing the good news in Christ? Is it a matter of words or deeds? Is it a matter of personal effort or the mysterious work of the Spirit? Maybe it's all of the above and more? Maybe it is not some of the above?

In *Life of the Beloved: Spiritual Living in a Secular World*, Henri Nouwen tried to write about faith and spirituality for his doubting, secular friends. His friends weren't persuaded. And while Nouwen was mortified by their negative response he finally came to the conclusion, "maybe I don't have to become an apologist for God's existence and the religious meaning of life."[25] But if that is the case, what should one be?

However one wishes to play with words the bottom line is most clear: We are to be the bearers of the secret of the Reign of God, we are to be witnesses to the goodness of God's grace in Christ, we are to be lovers of humanity, and we are to be those who seek to serve others.

All of this does not mean that it's all a matter of faith and not of understanding. We can speak about the God who creates. We may speak about the God who set Hebrew slaves free. We must speak about the God of the prophets who cry out on behalf of the poor. And we should speak about the Christ who takes humanity's sin to himself and grants forgiveness and the blessing of his Spirit.

But a true apologetic is not simply a matter of explanation. It is also a matter of the birth of faith. The mystery of God's Spirit's opening the heart and understanding is the very genesis of the discovery of faith.

The Word

Where the written Word and the Living Word meet

THE WESTERN WORLD has become increasingly skeptical regarding matters of faith and belief. Talk about a God beyond this world and life after death is seen as highly speculative, and by some as infantile. Of course, talk of faith and belief is usually tolerated; after all, we do live in a multicultural and pluralistic world. But such talk need not be taken too seriously. It reflects only one's personal and subjective preference.

However, the sense that there is or may be a God arises not only from one's inner world. Whether this sense comes from an existential sense of personal loneliness, a profound inner need, or from a sense of wonderment, it matters little.

An awareness of God may also come in many other ways: from seeing the beauty of nature, the averting of some crisis, a dream or a vision. The love of God may also be sensed through the kindness of another human being.

But there is another source for knowing about God: the Word. Saying this so simply is not in any way to suggest that the Bible is a self-evident revelation of God for every reader. Some readers think Scripture is simply great literature. Others think it's mere mythology.

But for many throughout the ages, the Bible is held to be the book in which God is revealed and the reading of which brings us closer to God and helps us to understand who God is and the nature of his way with us.

Central to this compilation of books is the revelation of Jesus Christ, Son of God, Son of Man, who reveals and embodies who God is and who is believed to be God incarnate.

The story of the Christ is one of subjection, suffering, and death. It is also the story of the One who loves fully, forgives graciously, embraces all, and brings spiritual life and hope to all who embrace him as God's gift to humankind.

Thus the written word is all about the Living Word. Words on pages point to the great self-giving of God in the Word made flesh. Mere words, and as such the humiliation of the word, reveal the even greater humiliation of the Living Word, God's Son, in human form.

Words ever so fragile, words so easily disregarded or dismissed, are the way God chooses to engage us. And in case we are inclined to think that mere words amount to little, God has embodied that word in Jesus Christ. Christ becomes the visible and substantial Word. A Word that spells deed. A Word that is active. A Word that can make one whole!

Henri Nouwen reminds us that "We need to wait together to keep each other at home spiritually, so that when the Word comes it can become flesh in us. That is why the book of God is always in the midst of those who gather. We read the Word so that the Word can become flesh and have a whole new life in us."[26] Indeed! This is no mere Word. It is a life-giving and life-transforming Word. A Word that lives in us through the Spirit, reorienting us to new ways of being. Ways that have to do with forgiveness, peacemaking, reconciliation, and healing.

In the mystery of faith a Word can open up a new world. In the brooding presence of the Spirit a Word can transform us. In the power of the Word made flesh a Word can heal us.

Purpose
Where faith and action meet

COMING TO FAITH IN GOD is the beginning of a very long journey. It is not, as some put it, a final homecoming. This journey at the same time moves us in a number of directions. It invites us into a fuller knowing of God and being known by God. It also opens the door to a greater self-knowing in the light of God's love for us. Furthermore, it invites us into growing into community, where we share life together as members of the household of faith. And finally, the journey calls us to find our place in the world as servants of the Reign of God.

These are not separate journeys. They are interrelated. The vertical leads to the horizontal. Growth in the life of God leads to self-growth, which empowers us for community building. And being part of the community of faith means that in solidarity with one another we can be a sacrament to the world.

This is a very broad frame in which we are called to live and serve as God's pilgrim people. But God's purposes for us also become more specific and more focused.

Some are called to marriage, while others believe that God leads them to a life of singleness. Some are called to serve the church, others the wider community. It matters not. One's status and role in life are important, but the greater determinative has to do with the way in which we live our lives and shape our roles.

The pulse beat of the Christian life is to honor God, point to the Christ who takes away the sin of the world, and live in the Spirit who sustains us and makes all things new.

Henri Nouwen asks "how radically new my life would be if I were willing to move beyond blaming to proclaiming the works of God in our midst."[27] He is right.

To live the heartbeat of the biblical story means that obstacles need to be overcome. We all have our fears. We so readily get side-tracked. Other things crowd in. Our vision of life in Christ through the Spirit gets easily dimmed. We are capable of compromise. Our love may grow weak. Our courage may fail us.

Again and again we need to be drawn back to the central purpose of our existence. Simply put, it is nothing other than this: Having been made in God's image, we are made to live in and for God. And to be in God is to be in relationship with the Son, the Redeemer; and with the Spirit, the animator of all things who gives life, wholeness, and renewal.

Out of this purpose we can live joyful, sacramental, and sacrificial lives. Heart and head come together as we seek to discern the direction of our lives, the purposes of God for our time, and the general and specific tasks and roles to which we have been called.

The heart infuses the head with passion and motivation. The head guides the heart in making particular priorities and commitments. But the central motif of the story remains the same: As those graced by God's goodness we seek to bring the blessings of God to our world in faith, prayer, and service.

Listening
Where reflection and obedience meet

THERE CAN BE A DYNAMIC RELATIONSHIP between experience and reflection. We experience the goodness or the purgation of God, and we then want to understand God's wonderful and difficult way with us.

Conversely, we can read the pages of Scripture and the wisdom of the saints, theologians, and great leaders of the church, and be so inspired that we seek to emulate and enter into the vision set out before us.

But at the heart of both of these movements is the posture of listening. This is the place where the longing heart and seeking mind meet.

Listening is the antidote to the impetuous heart and the closed mind. It is the invitation to the slow pace and to the open space. Listening in Christian spirituality is listening in many directions. It is listening to our inner life, it is listening to God's voice in Scripture; it is listening to the promptings of the Spirit; and it is listening to our world in all its goodness, pain, and idolatry. And as we noted above, it is also listening to the voices of the church's exemplary sons and daughters of the faith.

Listening defines us as much as our doing. In listening we acknowledge our need for the Other. In listening we shape our humility. In listening we create the seedbed for a life of purpose and action.

Just as receiving is the first movement of the Christian life, rather than giving, so listening is the basic movement of Christian spirituality. It is out of listening that other things can flow. Henri Nouwen reminds us that "obedience is about an experience of real listening to God." He continues, "I am deeply convinced that great renewal will develop whenever we enter into solitude together to discover how God is calling us."[28]

We tend not to do any of our listening well. We often fail to listen to our bodies and thus overwork them. We find the practice of solitude difficult and so fail to listen to our inner being and the voice of the Spirit. And an attentive reading of Scripture often eludes us because we are too busy with using the Bible for our own ends.

As for a careful listening to our world, we are often simply overwhelmed and tuned out. So much pain and conflict! So much poverty and injustice! We can't cope, and so we turn the dial.

But a careful listening can reorient us, center us, sustain us, and give direction for the journey. In listening to the wisdom of God we can regain a vision of what is finally central and important. The wisdom of God centers us, and provides the frame and inspiration by which we live.

In listening to the wisdom of God through the nudging of the Spirit who goes before us, we are given focus, purpose, direction. Here, obedience becomes our happy response.

In listening to our inner being we celebrate God's way with us and acknowledge our vulnerability, waywardness, and need. And in listening to our world we see the signs of God's goodness, pray for the Reign of God to come more fully, and live a life of love and service to others.

Trinity
Where faith and communion meet

ONE CAN NEVER COMPLAIN that there is not enough in the Christian faith that is intellectually challenging: the nature of God, the wonderment of creation, the mystery of the Incarnation. The list could go on and on. But one of the most challenging aspects of the Christian faith is the doctrine of the Trinity.

Henri Nouwen speaks about the Trinity as follows: "the Father loves the Son and pours himself out in the Son. The Son is loved by the Father and returns all he is to the Father. The Spirit is love itself, eternally embracing the Father and the Son."[29]

The creeds of Christendom have expressed this doctrine in more complex language. And in much simpler language we could speak of God as a community of persons: Father, Son, and Holy Spirit.

None of the above expressions are without difficulty since we are seeking to express that God is One and that God has three modes of being.

But why is this important? you may ask. At a number of levels the answer is simple enough. The Bible speaks of the Father; Christ, the Son of God; and the Holy Spirit. So it's not surprising that we want to understand their relationship. It is also reasonable to assert that our understanding of God, who is at the center of the Christian story, has huge implications for the way in which we understand other parts of the story.

If God were a lone monad in the universe, or if God were merely our own self-projection, or if God were only a tribal deity, this would have huge implications for how we would live the Christian faith.

But the eternal God is a communion of community, a God of mutual self-giving. And this has implications for us. Coming to Christian faith is entering into this love relationship between Father, Son, and Holy Spirit. This is the ultimate welcome and befriending. It is also the ultimate homecoming. It is entering into the circle of love, mutuality, and care of the Trinity that defines our identity, reconfigures our life of fear and insecurity, and sustains a journey of growth in Christ-likeness and service to the world.

The restless one enters this circle of friendship. The bruised and wounded one is welcomed into this community of love and well-being. Coming home to this, God makes us whole.

Who God is, is what we are to be like. What God does in his love, forgiveness, welcome, and healing, we are to extend to others as the fruit and overflow of our lives.

This communion, this mutuality, this love, this welcome, we are to reflect in the communities of faith that seek to be a witness to the beauty of this God. Thus the doctrine of the Trinity is no dry-as-sawdust doctrine. It is a living statement of who God is and what God does and what we are to become as servants of the Reign of God.

Through Death
Where faith and transformation meet

THE CHRISTIAN LIFE IS ONE OF FAITH seeking understanding. It is also a life of trust in the face of mystery. And part of that mystery is the embrace of the strange idea that death is the way of life.

Everything within our fragile being would want to suggest that the opposite is true, that death is the end of life. And the whole of our contemporary culture affirms this. Death is a topic to be avoided. Instead, let us live life to the fullest, with death cast into the shadow lands.

The Christian story, however, has a very different melody line. And this melody is no dirge; it is a joyous oratorio. This line is that God's way is the embrace of death in order that new life might come. This, after all, is the heart of the Easter story.

Henri Nouwen begins this amazing story this way: I am invited to believe "that in and through Christ's death has become the way by which the Spirit of truth [and life] comes to us."[30] This somewhat awkward sentence is the invitation to this awkward mystery.

The starting point of this mystery is that God's way is fundamentally different from ours. We believe life begets life and that death—any form of death—is a diminution, a deprivation, a mere negation that must be valiantly resisted.

The Christian story sings very differently. It is in and through the death of Christ that new life is offered to us. Death begets life.

The Christian life, then, is not simply one that embraces this truth that in the death of the One, life is offered for all. The Christian life also involves this becoming the script for our own lives.

What this means is not only a reference to the great transition where in death we hope for the resurrection in the life to come. It also means that life is to be lived with many dyings.

The impulse for these dyings is not a morbid self-negation. Instead, the impulse comes from a joyous following of the way of Christ. For the sake of Christ, and in the name of love, we embrace the way of relinquishment and even suffering in order that life might come to others.

Thus, from a selfish self-protection and self-preoccupation we move, empowered by the Spirit, to a self-giving that seeks to do God's good to others. This movement may even involve our taking to ourselves the pain of others in the privacy of prayer and in acts of care.

The great surprise in all of this is that this strange way may not only be life-giving for others but also for ourselves. In the many steps of a little dying our own transformation is furthered and enhanced.

While our culture in celebrating youth seeks to negate the reality of death, the Christian faith moves in the opposite direction: Dying to our own ways through the grace of Christ opens windows to living and celebrating a new life.

Transformation
Where the old and the new meet

AT THE HEART OF THE CHRISTIAN STORY lies a threefold plot: All was created good and well; through our disobedience and folly we distorted this pristine setting; and God with persistent love seeks to bring about a full mending, healing, and restoration.

Put in more theological language we are speaking about creation, chaos, and the new creation. The contours of this new creation are most clearly revealed in the person and work of Christ, who has made the way for all things to become new and to be restored to God's ultimate vision of *shalom*.

The biblical story speaks not only of new heavens and earth as the grandest frame of this restoration, but also of humans' receiving a new heart and mind. In the words of Henri Nouwen: "You so much want to give me a home, a sense of belonging, a place to dwell, a shelter where I feel protected and a refuge in which I feel safe." In this welcome, Nouwen explains, is the invitation to "come and know that I [the Lord God] have come to give you a new heart and a new spirit."[31]

Is such a thing possible? And how may we understand such a transformation?

Its possibility is premised on the nature of God's restorative love, and this is revealed in the long story of God's way with humankind. That the Creator can renew the creation is self-evident.

But how do we understand all of this? Can we really be transformed? And what does it mean that we may receive a new heart and a new spirit?

What we are speaking of here is the gift of an inner transformation that changes our inner rhythms and motivations and the whole direction of our lives. In biblical language it is as if one is born all over again and that one becomes a new person.

So how does this happen? There are different ways of saying much the same thing. It happens through a questing for a greater good and wholeness. It happens when we surprisingly encounter the greater good. And it happens in mysterious ways when the greater good grows within us. And, of course, none of these possibilities is exhaustive.

Within a Christian framework, this revelation or encounter with the greater good is an experience of the embracing love of God in Christ through the mediating work of the Holy Spirit. In this we realize that our way is folly, our own goodness is fatally flawed, and the meaning and direction of our lives are without ultimate purpose. Moreover, we are aware of a foundational lostness.

In this encounter we recognize that Christ has healing for us, that to live in the way of Christ gives us true purpose, and that with Christ there is a homecoming that overcomes our existential aloneness.

A new heart and spirit spring from this spiritual encounter. And by our growing in the wisdom and way of Christ through the Spirit, new ways of thinking, hoping, dreaming, living, loving, and serving grow in us.

HEART
TO HEART

The Wonderment and Responsibility of Friendship and Community

IN OUR WORLD many people live with deep anxieties. While many worry about security and economic well-being, the greater worries continue to center around identity and relational issues.

The "Who am I?" question and "Who can I trust and depend on?" cry remain fundamental issues of human existence. And on the heels of these matters there remains the ever-painful question of community and the quest of "Where am I truly at home?"

That these are burning matters for so many comes as no surprise given the movement in urban life. Not only do our cities and neighborhoods constantly change, but so do our jobs and where we chose to live. And our families and marriages, in this kind of setting, are hardly stable and constant.

Moreover, in our multicultural and multireligious world we are ever more faced with diversity. This diversity pressures us regarding who we are and in what ways we are not like "them." But then we are also not so sure whether we like being who we are.

Little wonder, therefore, that in our very fragmented way of life we yearn for community. In the fluidity of our many contacts with people, we long for deeper relationships and friendships.

Sadly, the church is often not seen as providing answers for this state of affairs. Not only does the church not appear to be attractive, it is seen as equally fragmented and as being without friendship and community.

That the church should be otherwise is everywhere evident on the pages of Scripture. The Bible knows a lot about friendship and building community.

The restoration of friendship with God in Christ provides the impulse for building relationships of love and care among each other and for building faith communities beyond gender, social, ethnic, and economic differences. The New Testament vision has always been for a new humanity in Christ.

That the converse should also be true is one of the biggest challenges facing the contemporary church, namely, that such love, acceptance, and friendship should be offered in the church that people are drawn to friendship with God.

Henri Nouwen deeply struggled with all of these issues. He sought the renewal of congregations. He longed for deep friendships, and he sought to build community wherever he found himself.

None of this readily fell into place for him. In friendship he often moved between being too generous and too demanding. And he often expected of others what they simply could not give.

In his experience of community he sought to build community with his students in the academy, in his sojourn in monasteries, and in his participation in the parish church. But he most fully found community in his participation in the L'Arche Daybreak community in Toronto, Canada, serving those with physical and intellectual disabilities.

In some sense, Nouwen was always searching, and in every sense homecoming eluded him until the final blessing of death. So, as we enter the vision of the biblical narrative and journey with Nouwen, we too may find ourselves positioned between the hunger of our need, the vulnerability of our relationships and communities, and the hope of final homecoming and fulfillment.

Whether the journey is easy or difficult, we are invited to the wonderment and responsibility of friendship and community.

Fragile Communities
Experiencing grace in the midst of brokenness

THE HUMAN BEING seems to be characterized by insatiable needs. For many these needs have to do with inner well-being. And key among these needs is the desire to be known and loved in the midst of family, friends, and community.

As a result, we hope for, and sometimes demand, much of our relationships with others. But friendship is not built well when it springs from a wounded emptiness that knows only the language of demand. Relationships are instead built on the gift of commonality where both are givers and receivers in the gift of grace and the practice of goodness and care. Thus, reciprocity lies at the heart of relationship building.

There are many implications that flow from this most basic of observations. One such implication is that we cannot place our hope in what the other will do for us in friendship and community. We can only hope in the goodness that God gives in the midst of life together.

Nouwen came to this realization during his time at the Abbey of Genesee in upstate New York. He writes, "[A] monastery is not built to solve problems, but to praise the Lord in the midst of them."[32] To which we could add in a similar vein, communities are not created to provide for my security, but to find a common life in the grace and forgiveness of Christ. Furthermore, friendships don't come into being to assuage our loneliness, but to help us support one another in common commitments and in the common journey of life.

It is ever so easy to operate with inappropriate expectations. And often what we hope for is the quick answer, or the easy road, or the magical relief. But friendships, families, and communities are all made of a fragile texture. These networks of relationship require love, care, and nurture. They require commitment for the long haul of building and maintaining.

These configurations of life together call for the practice of solidarity, mutuality, and generosity. And laced throughout every membrane is the giving of forgiveness and the reception of grace.

Though we are invited to build friendships, families, and communities, they are also a gift. Within a Christian framework, they are gifts of grace. This means that in Christ through the Holy Spirit we are made one and thus live life together in faith and hope, in care and commitment, in forgiveness and goodness.

But none of this can be cast in idyllic terms. This is no utopian vision. Communities in and through Christ will always be vulnerable. And friendships will always be fragile.

Thus, our major focus should be not to find easy answers but to journey together, not to escape from difficulties but to join others on the journey, not simply to have our needs met but to live with others in the commonality of grace.

For the Other
Experiencing openness to outsiders

TO HAVE GENUINE AND LASTING FRIENDSHIPS, to have a family of care and warmth, and to have a faith community of nurture and formation is to be blessed indeed! None of this is asking for too much. It is amazing how much support and encouragement we need in the journey of life and faith.

But whether we have much or little, we always run the danger of clinging to what we have and to make the gifts of friends, family, and community exclusive rather than inclusive. In other words, we fail in the politics of radical openness to the other and in the practice of solidarity and hospitality.

The movement of the biblical narrative is always the movement from particularity to universality. Abram was chosen and blessed, but in order to be a blessing to the nations. Israel, God's elect, was called to be a light to the nations. The church, the people of God, graced by Christ and empowered by the Spirit, is challenged to be a servant, sign, and sacrament of the Kingdom of God.

Nouwen, in reflecting on the story of Jesus, notes, "You became a refugee in Egypt to show us your solidarity with all who are driven from their homes," and "[Y]ou went the long road of suffering and death to show us that you did not want to remain an outsider even in the most painful of all human experiences."[33] And, we may add: You, Lord Jesus, became one of us so that we may follow your example to be in solidarity with all humanity. Or to sharpen the focus: You, Lord Jesus, became the suffering One, inviting us to suffering on behalf of others.

The basic motif of the biblical story is that the gifts, blessings and goodness that come our way from God's beneficence are gifts for sharing. Others, therefore, are to be welcomed into the circle of our relationships and into the heart of our communities.

This does not mean that we do not protect and guard the sacredness of our relationships and communities. We don't offer these to others in order for these to be harmed or destroyed. But we do in faith and love risk our relationships and communities in order for these to become a grace and goodness for others.

As former strangers and aliens from the heart of God, but having been welcomed "home" to the love and grace of God, we now desire to live in welcome to others who seek peace with God. We also want to extend the welcome we have received from God to others who are the strangers and the marginalized in our society.

Thus the welcome of God leads to welcome of neighbor, including the neighbor as a marginal person. And so the mark of health in our relationships and faith communities and in society as a whole, is not the way we cling to what we have but the way in which we steward these things.

What we hold tightly and for ourselves does not grow in greater enrichment but diminishes us. Enrichment lies in sharing with a thankful heart. The way of such a heart is the way of joy that so much has been received, therefore much may be given.

Working Together
Experiencing the joining of hearts and hands

CHRISTIAN COMMUNITY is never simply about providing a place of nurture and care for its participants. While that is part of the story, it is only a chapter, not the whole book. Community is also a place of service and of corporate witness. It is particularly this last point that I wish to explore in this reflection.

When Nouwen was part of the Daybreak community, he would take a core member, a person with physical and/or intellectual disabilities, with him on his various speaking engagements. Regarding this practice, Nouwen made the following observation: "Whenever we minister together, it is easier for people to recognize that we do not come here in our own name, but in the name of the Lord Jesus who sent us."[34]

There is much that one could say about this. The most basic is not simply that Nouwen sought to give people with a disability a visibility and a voice—important though that is—but that Nouwen accented the value and importance of common witness.

A faith community seeks to celebrate the theme of life together, and related to that, the theme of communal service and witness to the world. Christian service should not be the burden of the isolated Christian but the joy of opening a life together in Christ to the neighborhood, to others.

Thus, being together is already working together. The two are interrelated. Being together can issue in working together, but working together can sacramentally solidify our being together. This working together is not only for the internal well-being of the faith community but also for service to the world as sign of the Kingdom of God.

Our service and witness to the world ought to be a communal one. The community is an embodiment of the Word of God. The community of faith is a community in mission.

Why is this important? Because no solitary individual can give adequate witness and testimony to the God as community: Father, Son, and Holy Spirit. Because no individual can adequately reflect the varied wisdom and glory of God. It is only people in relationship in Christ who can show something of the way and wisdom of God in our world.

The idea of being together and working together in order to show the glory of God places a significant challenge on the community of faith. The most fundamental is that what we say and what we are must, therefore, be integrated. We can't speak of a God who brings people together when our churches are racially divided. We can't speak of the forgiveness of God if our communities are judgmental. We can't celebrate the God who heals if we do not know God's healing presence amongst us.

If the contemporary church seeks once again to become a significant voice in our society, it will need to recover a communal voice that comes from a communal vision and a communal sharing of life.

Reconciliation and Healing
Experiencing the grace of community building

No FRIENDSHIP, RELATIONSHIP, FAMILY, OR COMMUNITY can continue to be well without lots of care. Good things need sustenance, and this is required throughout the entire journey, not simply at the beginning.

Some relationships and communities start well because so much thought, love, care, and prayer were put into them. But the idea that later on things can simply coast along is woefully wrongheaded. No community can exist and continue healthy in that way.

One of the bread and butter issues in community building is the facilitation of ongoing reconciliation among members of the community—a reconciliation that leads to greater healing and wholeness. For some readers this comes as a big surprise. Aren't people already reconciled? Aren't they sharing a common vision? Have they not committed themselves to sharing a common life?

The answer to this is, yes . . . but. The very nature of life together calls for processes that help us to remain connected. The erection of barriers, the building up of misunderstandings, the movement of jealousy or hurt or harbored resentment also occur in faith communities, whether those be the regular church or extended households or special faith communities such as L'Arche.

Henri Nouwen writes clearly out of his own experience: "Every time I have an opportunity to create understanding between people and foster movements of healing, forgiving, and uniting, I will try to do it, even though I might be criticized as too soft, too bending, too appeasing."[35]

The work of reconciliation, forgiveness, peacemaking, joining, building, uniting, and moving a community forward in a common vision of love and service is no easy task. It is a gift. And the outworking of such a charism is grace.

In community, persons with such gifts are needed. They are not always well understood, for the ability to draw people together in community is not a matter of management expertise. Rather, it is the fruit of a gifting and formation springing from a mystical vision born of prayer.

What I mean by this is that the experience of reconciliation and forgiveness cannot come from any form of duress. It can come from inner transformation. And the power of this transformation can come only from the presence of the Holy Spirit working mysteriously among us. In community there is the need for people who can discern this work of the Spirit and can create space for the Spirit's work to erupt, break down barriers, and draw us into forgiveness and peace-making.

Communities of faith are, therefore, fundamentally communities of forgiveness. As such, they are communities of healing when blockages to growth in trust, hope, and faith are removed.

Those who carry both the gift and the spiritual burden to see this happen are people of discernment and prayer. They are the healers of relationships. They build community!

Contemplation
Experiencing attentiveness to God and friend

WHEN WE THINK OF THE GIFT AND BLESSING of friendship and community we most readily think about the importance of communicating and relating well. We tend not to think about the importance of contemplation. And yet, contemplation is key to building friendship and community.

Contemplation is one of the key practices in Christian spirituality. It is a grace gift that comes to us as fruit of the practice of solitude and prayer. The practice of stillness and waiting provides the space for the contemplative experience. And this experience is to come to a greater awareness of God, ourselves, and others.

In contemplation we may see and hear what normally eludes us. Typically, so much passes us by because, caught up in the values of . our world, we are ever so busy and often so inattentive, even with people with whom we live or work.

Henri Nouwen makes the observation "that our most private times of contemplation are not only good for us individually, but are also, in the final analysis, a service to the whole community."[36]

Clearly, two meanings are intended here. The first is that, to the degree that contemplation brings goodness, grace, and insight to me, to that extent it can become an overflow blessing to others. Second, there are communal dimensions to the contemplative experience, and as such these are blessings for the whole community. Let me elaborate on this latter dimension.

Contemplation is waiting in solitude, prayer, and expectancy. It is attentiveness to God. But it is also attentiveness to what is going on inside of me, and since what I am thinking about or am concerned with is not only about me but also others, it is obvious that in the contemplative experience others are also in the picture.

While the contemplative experience begins in stillness it often ends in peace, or worship, or insight, or prayer. Thus in the quiet place I may gain insights into my relationships and issues and concerns with others, including those in my family or community. The fruit of this may result in a greater concern for someone, or a renewed constructive attitude, or a greater prayerfulness.

Thus, contemplation is not simply about God and me. It is also about God and the community of faith of which I am a part. It follows, then, that community is not simply about serving, it is also about prayer. Community is not only about connecting, it is also about withdrawal. It is not only about doing, but also about interceding.

Healthy community is not only about externalization but also about internalization. It is as much about the inner life as it is about relationships and seeking to serve the wider society.

A Little Dying

*Experiencing the movement from narcissism
to communal care*

OUR WORLD CELEBRATES THE INDIVIDUAL. Our way of life is all about the freedom, security, welfare, and development of the individual. This way of life is all about the autonomous self. The individual is seen as separate from others and independent in relation to others. This emphasis has led to unhealthy forms of individualism and narcissism.

In contrast, in the biblical story, the human being is always seen as a person in relationship—with God and others. This is a small reflection of the mystery of the Trinity—God as a community of persons. Thus human beings made in God's image are made for relationship both vertically and horizontally—we are created for God and for each other.

To a greater or lesser degree these two visions of what it means to be human are "at war" within us. There is the propensity toward individualism and selfishness, and there is the call of the gospel to see ourselves in relationship with others and to love others as we love ourselves.

Nouwen knew this inner turmoil. He writes of experiencing "a series of little deaths in which we are asked to release many forms of clinging and to move increasingly from needing others to living for them."[37]

It needs to be pointed out that the goal is not to become independent of others. The movement of life in relationship is to cease from being wholly self-preoccupied. Thus the movement is toward inter-dependence. It is living the rhythm of receiving and giving, of giving and receiving.

The movement of living for others is not a form of self-negation. It is the overflow of a life that has been kissed by God. It is blessing others as we have been blessed.

Extending ourselves toward others cannot be done well when driven by the need to be needed or when driven by subtle forms of control. However, self-giving must not wait until we are wholly motivationally pure. We will always be the wounded healers and the vulnerable givers.

But there is joy in being there for others. There can be joy in service. There is goodness for the giver in giving. The movement in giving is always to be life-giving. It is about the well-being and enhancement of the other.

As a result, giving must always be a discerning giving. Is the other open to receive a gift? Is this good timing? Will it empower the other?

God in Christ has given us life. This is a gift that frees. It has enabled us. We are called to follow this example. The many little dyings implicit in our move from self-preoccupation and narcissism to caring for others are deaths that are really a form of resurrection that gives life to all.

Living the Paschal Mystery
Experiencing resurrection in the midst of death

THERE IS LITTLE DOUBT that the greater the depth of a relationship—whether it be family, friend, colleague, or church member—the greater the possibility that such a relationship will lead to suffering. The ones we love are also the ones we suffer. The ones we deeply care about also draw us into their suffering. And these relationships, when they get into difficulties or disintegrate, can cause us the deepest hurt.

Therefore our experience of meaningful relationships and of community are not only places of joy and uplifting, they are also places of painful transformation. They are places that call us into living the paschal mystery.

The paschal mystery lies at the very heart of the biblical story. Prefigured in the Exodus Passover meal and more fully expressed in the death and resurrection of Christ and the first Eucharistic celebration, the paschal mystery speaks to us on several levels. First, it speaks of the innocent suffering One taking upon himself the load of our guilty suffering. Second, it reminds us that out of suffering and death, new life can spring forth. And finally, we are invited into suffering for the sake of the other, for the community. It is particularly this last point that I wish to explore further.

To go directly to the heart of the matter: Nothing life-giving, beautiful, or empowering comes about at no cost. It usually comes into being through painful transformations.

The tulip bursts forth from winter's dark and damp earth. The Australian jacaranda, with its shimmering purple-blue, adorns a denuded tree. And friendships form because someone was willing to love, to risk, to hope, to reach out. Communities grow because people love, pray, serve, and are willing, at cost to themselves, to carry the community in hope and love.

Nouwen makes the above poignantly clear: "Just as the ground can only bear fruit as it is broken by the plough, so too, our own lives can only be fruitful when they have been opened through passion, that is, suffering."[38]

Our empty culture promises us the opposite. You can be and have everything at no cost, although you will need to pay later. We are often promised fulfillment without pain, meaning without mystery, and happiness without needing to give.

The gospel promises something quite different. It invites us to "die" to our own ways and to embrace the way of Christ. It challenges our individualism and invites us into community. It calls us to service rather than self-seeking. It calls us to the ways of peace rather than aggression and war.

And finally, and possibly most fundamentally, the story of God invites us into a willing suffering for the sake of the other. The call is to lay down our lives for the life of the other.

Called to Community
Experiencing the joy and challenge of life together

FAMILY, THE CHURCH, AND MONASTIC OR RELIGIOUS ORDERS are generally regarded as varying forms of community. But there are many other alternative forms of Christian community: L'Arche and L'Abri are two well-known other examples.

Christian community can be built anywhere: in the local church and neighborhood, in the workplace, in the university. Anywhere where we live and work, community can be built.

So what do we mean by Christian community? The central core has to do with sharing life together in Christ. Nouwen puts it more specifically: "We cannot live in intimate communion with Jesus without being sent to our brothers and sisters who belong to that same humanity that Jesus has accepted as his own. Thus intimacy manifests itself as solidarity and solidarity as intimacy."[39] Or to put that much more basically, being linked to Christ by faith in the Spirit means that we are also linked to one another as members of the body of Christ, the community of faith.

Community can have varying levels of commitment and intentionality. By way of example, there is quite a difference in participation if one only attends a one-hour worship service or if one also lives in an extended household or intentional community where much of life is shared.

Community at this greater level of intentionality involves sharing a common faith, a common set of purposes for being together, a commonality of place, common practices in terms of a life together, and a common mission or vision.

While some Christians live this level of intentionality, for the majority this seems out of their reach or maybe even undesirable. But this way of life needs to be reconsidered, particularly since our consumer Christianity with its minimal commitments and its many options is not faring well. The form of Christianity that predominates in the Western world is not a very credible Christianity and is making little impact.

So why consider more intentional forms of being the people of God, the body of Christ? First, the biblical narrative shows that God has always been intent on building a people. Second, Jesus formed a community of disciples. Third, the early church as households of faith shared life together. And fourth, forms of intentional community have existed throughout the church's long journey.

But the more fundamental reason is that Jesus calls us into the joy, challenges, and responsibilities of working out our love for him through love for brothers and sisters in the faith. And this life together of love, care, and sharing becomes the base for our witness and service to the world.

Our world is tired of words and needs to see the embodied word of God in faith communities of celebration and service that extend a welcome to the world. A welcome that says, come and taste and see that the Lord is good and his mercy is toward all.

The Caring Friend
Experiencing the being there of companionship

IN THE MIDST OF OUR EVERYDAY INDIVIDUALISM and the search for an independent lifestyle—a lifestyle of such independence for some that marriage and having children is seen as a major infringement and long-term vocational commitments as a sheer impossibility— the search for community and friendships continues unabated.

So what about our friendships then, whatever our lifestyle? What may we hope for? What kinds of relationships do we work toward?

I believe that the place to start is with the simple acknowledgment that friendship, while a process, is most fundamentally a gift. One can put much into a relationship with a certain person and still this person may never become a friend. Conversely, a chance encounter may lead to a developing and deepening friendship.

A friend is a person we know, like, and trust. An intimate friend is one with whom this relationship has deepened over time and with whom we are willing to share much of our inner concerns. To have friends on this level of relationship is a great gift in terms of companionship, shared wisdom, common celebration, and sense of social solidarity.

All of this is not to say that friendships cannot be problematical. Friendship may be betrayed. Friendship may create dependency. Friendship, no matter how deep and meaningful, can fall apart. But one of the recurring difficulties in many friendships has to do with the whole realm of expectations. While we can expect too little and thus stultify a friendship, we may expect too much and thus put pressure on the relationship that it cannot bear or sustain.

Henri Nouwen, who experienced much difficulty in some of his friendships because he expected more than they could give, writes out of his own agonizing journey. He points out that we do need friends who "not-caring, not-healing [can] face us with the reality of our powerlessness." He goes on to say, such a person "is a friend who cares."[40]

This is a very important and relevant matter. In the final analysis we don't live the solutions of life. Instead, we live the mystery of life. The whole gamut of ambiguity is part of the human experience. A good friend, therefore, is not the fix-it person. Rather, a friend is willing to journey with us in our confusion, or our pain, or our powerlessness. And to travel life in such a way is no easy matter, for we do want to help, and we don't want to see a person we care for suffer.

A friend who is willing to journey with us in our darkness and difficulty is a true friend, indeed. It is not the healing friend but the being-there friend who is making the greater commitment, for such a person has to face his or her own powerlessness as well as the pain and difficulty of the other.

A true companion—in the vulgar Latin—is one who simply eats bread with another. A true friend is one who eats the bread of affliction with another, thus making such a friendship a truly sacramental and Eucharistic reality.

A Community of Brokenness
Experiencing the vulnerability of the human condition

IF THERE IS ANYTHING THAT CHARACTERIZES OUR FAMILIES, our relationships, and our communities, it is the word *vulnerability*. We may feel somewhat certain about the stability and permanence of some human institutions, such as a great university or a major corporation, or the political stability of our particular country (although in the twenty-first century these all seem far more tenuous than in previous decades), but families, friendships, and communities of faith are by their very nature fragile.

One of the main reasons they are so fragile is that they don't carry major institutional infrastructure to safeguard them. Relationships and communities exist by the ongoing goodwill of their members.

While communities of faith can rely on the goodness of God and the sustaining presence of the Holy Spirit, this grace does not make them immune from the most fundamental of all human realities— the ongoing brokenness of human existence. Therefore, Henri Nouwen does well in this reminder: "When we say that the church is a body, we refer not only to the holy and faultless body made Christ-like through baptism and Eucharist, but also to the broken bodies of all the people who are its members. Only when we keep both these ways of thinking and speaking together can we live in the church as true followers of Jesus."[41]

And so it is, no matter how much we may wish things were different. The community of faith consists of people on a journey, a people under reconstruction. A faith community is a work in progress. This community, while a community of worship, teaching, love, fellowship, and service, is most fundamentally a community in waiting. It is a community that prays that God's kingdom, reign, and presence will be more fully manifest among them.

Faith communities are not the domain of the religious specialist, the utopian dreamer, the perfected ones, those living a higher form of spirituality. Instead, they are the province of those touched by the grace of God who are seeking to grow in holiness, wholeness, and discipleship.

While the signs of grace are present in a faith community in worship, work, and sacrament, the signs of weakness and brokenness are evident in the need for forgiveness, healing, and renewal. As a result, faith communities can be the most open and welcoming of all places. Here not the social mask but genuine humility becomes the operative reality.

Because communities of faith are communities of brokenness there is the presence of prayer, the gift of encouragement, the blessing of nurture, and the goodness of sharing together in the common activities of daily life.

As communities in waiting everything can become sacramental: the baking of bread, sharing a meal, foot-washing. Living in the light of what God will yet do, hope becomes the dominant theme. Hope is inherently vulnerable, the opposite of "having arrived."

HEART
DARKNESS

Faith and Mystery in the Journeys of Doubt and the Dark Night of the Soul

THE THEME OF HEART DARKNESS tends not to be an important focus in the preaching and teaching ministry of the contemporary church. Being in great difficulty and facing deep challenges, the church has opted for sunnier themes. It has done this in the hope of making itself more attractive to present-day seekers.

The only accent that comes close to this important and varied topic is to speak of the darkness in which a person of non-faith lives. In other words, the alienation of one without faith in Christ is preached in the context of an invitation to embrace Christ for the forgiveness of sins and participation in the new life that Christ gives.

But there are other themes that also need careful attention. A person of faith can experience heart darkness in a disturbing variety of ways. These may well include the following: times of prayer-lessness, seasons of doubt regarding God's presence and goodness, being overwhelmed by life's problems and difficulties, the persistence of unhelpful patterns of thought and behavior, severe temptations, and the experience of the dark night of the soul.

The above is hardly an exhaustive list. Life's color and darkness are manifold; the mystery of goodness and evil are ever perplexing. And the journey of life and faith has many contours in the road.

I wish that at the beginning of my journey of faith in Christ more was said about the seasons of the spiritual life and the rhythms of a life of faith. I wish that I had not been given the impression that once I had come to faith in Christ everything was now well and things would simply get better. That they did not brought about several crises.

Heart darkness is not an aberration in the Christian life. It is part and parcel of the Christian's journey.

The most fundamental way in which heart darkness is a relevant topic is that every Christian continues to struggle with imperfection and waywardness, with areas of woundedness, and with specific temptations. Every Christian is on the way toward greater conformity to Christ. And every Christian stretches forward toward greater maturity and wholeness.

The more difficult contours of heart darkness have to do with the blight of doubt. For some, everything is affected. God, Scripture, church, prayer are all called into question. Often, times of doubt are sculpted by life's unexpected difficulties and trials. Hard things come our way, and we wonder why God did not protect us.

The more puzzling theme of heart darkness has to do with the experience of the dark night of the soul. Often suddenly and for seemingly no reason, God's presence becomes an eerie silence. And we are left wondering how we have failed or sinned, and we find it difficult to grope our way back to the comforting bosom of God's heart of love.

Henri Nouwen was no exception to this tapestry of difficulty. Despite his profound faith in Christ, his wealth of experience of support in the Christian community, and his many friends, admirers, and supporters, Nouwen wrote about his struggles of faith and life. His most agonizing times revolved around issues of security and identity. At one point his friends had to hold and care for him for days on end while he cried out his brokenness in prayer and lament.

While much of Nouwen's life journey consisted of an underlying struggle with his self-worth and identity, matters of sexual orientation and his commitment to celibacy proved agonizing at times for this servant of Christ. His poignant *The Inner Voice of Love: A Journey through Anguish and Freedom* was later published from Nouwen's diary of that time.

Losing What Was Given
Recognizing the fragility of grace

THE MOST BASIC MOVEMENT OF THE CHRISTIAN LIFE is that of receiving. We receive God's love in Christ. We receive the Holy Spirit; the Spirit is poured out upon us. We receive both grace and forgiveness.

But some of the good that has been given can also be lost. We don't always know how to hold well what has been granted to us. We fail to recognize some gifts; others we fritter away. I am not speaking about losing one's faith. I am talking about the possibility of the benefit of certain blessings being eroded.

After his accident—he was hit by a car while walking by the side of the road—and subsequent hospitalization, Henri Nouwen experienced a deepening of his faith that recognized the fragility of grace. It was as if he could see more clearly the purpose of prayer, love, and service. He seemed to have caught a fuller glimpse of the Kingdom of God and the purposes of God for our world.

He later wrote: "I have lost much of the peace and freedom that was given to me in the hospital. I regret it; I even grieve over it. Once again there are many people, many projects, many pulls. Never enough time and space to do it all and feel totally satisfied."[42]

In times of solitude, prayer, and reflection, and in times of "forced" rest and Sabbath, much goodness may be given to us. In the in-between spaces of our existence, as our hearts and minds are turned more attentively to God, we may see things that normally elude us, including things of the world of faith and of God's Spirit.

So often we don't know how to hold what was given and fail to consolidate the workings of God in our Sabbath spaces. We simply become busy again and forget.

One of the more subtle forms of heart darkness is the almost imperceptible movement of discouragement. We have had a sense of God's presence, our faith is revitalized, we are moved anew by the stirrings of the Spirit, our faith is strengthened, and our prayer is re-energized. And yet, this fades from view. We once again find ourselves walking the more mundane rhythms of our daily existence rather than experiencing "life in the Spirit."

Let me make a number of reflections on this scenario.

The first is that less may be lost than we fear. We did receive in times of blessing, food and drink for the journey of faith. Thankfulness rather than regret may be a better receptacle to hold the gifts of God.

Second, the particular framework in which we have received a blessing from God, for example a time of enforced stillness or inactivity, is the same framework we may need to repeat in smaller ways sacramentally to hold what was given. Remembrance and repetition are better vehicles for the goodness of God than a sense of loss that leads to discouragement.

Finally, the greater lesson is to hold and to receive God's good gifts both in our times of reflection and in the midst of our busyness.

Embracing Pain
Recognizing the folly of avoidance

I SUPPOSE IT IS GENERALLY TRUE TO SAY that many of us are hit-and-run people. Or to put that in other terms, we are often in denial and avoidance when we should be facing things, including areas of difficulty and hurt.

The run and avoid mentality seems to be part of the very genetic make-up of who we are as humans. The primal story of Adam and Eve's disobedience and hiding points in the same direction.

One of the factors that contribute to heart darkness is our propensity to rationalize, avoid, or suppress both the sinful and hurting parts of our lives. As a consequence, we are often over-burdened, we are blindsided in particular situations, and we become involved in strange compensatory behaviors.

It is reasonable to offer the opinion that the delicate fabric of our inner being was not made to carry so much undealt-with junk. We were made for peace and joy in our relationships, both with God and with each other. We were not made to carry indefinitely unresolved conflict and hurt.

One of the key ways forward is to acknowledge and face our woundedness and the difficulties of life. Nouwen suggests that "Those who do not run away from our pains but touch them with compassion bring healing and new strength. The paradox indeed is that the beginning of healing is in the solidarity with the pain."[43]

While some of our pain or difficulty may come from an accident or an illness, much of our pain is of a relational nature. We are hurt by what others say about us, have done to us, or have failed to say or do.

But there is other pain as well. Parents experience pain in watching their children suffer. Lovers experience pain when the beloved is in difficulty in some way. And all of us experience various kinds of hurt and difficulty as a result of the brokenness of our world, where so much good is often so badly marred by wrongdoing, stupidity, and maliciousness.

In addition, one pain that Christians carry is that of seeing family, friends, colleagues, and neighbors not being attracted to the love of God in Christ Jesus. At a more profound level, Christians carry pain because of the compromises they make, the lack of the church's vitality and spirituality, and identification with the deep grief in the heart of God for a world that fails to hear and heed the welcome of God.

Since pain is with us, how do we deal with it? A less than helpful way is to find blame. It is far more life-giving to forgive, where forgiveness is appropriate. But this only gets us part of the way.

One of our challenges is to deal with the cultural notion that we *deserve* no harm to come our way. But this is sheer unreality. Brokenness is a part of life. The deeper reality in facing our hurts and difficulties is to join with the suffering God. If God suffered in Christ, we who are in Christ are invited to join with this God. Thus, in God's presence we carry our suffering sacramentally, believing that in the embrace of suffering and in the "death" of suffering, God's new life will break forth among us.

Corrosion

Recognizing the impact of secularism

HAVING LIVED IN EUROPE, AUSTRALIA, NORTH AMERICA, AND ASIA, and having taught at an international graduate school of Christian studies, I have been struck by some fundamental differences between Christians from the First World and those from the Two-Thirds World.

The most basic difference is that Christians from the Majority World, unlike Westerners, have a far greater sense of the supernatural in daily affairs. Western Christians tend to be functional atheists, even though they believe in God. Third-World Christians believe much more in God's direct intervention with the world, and so they pray for healing and God's provision.

In the West, many Christians are quite discouraged. The church is not doing well, being pushed more and more to the margins of mainstream society. Maintaining one's faith is hard work, with often-meager results. And a life of witness and service often feels unproductive and somehow insignificant. Prayer is difficult and often unrewarding. To put it bluntly, God seems awfully distant, and the realities of our culture seem powerfully pervasive.

Henri Nouwen puts all this most clearly: "Secularism has entered deeply into our hearts, leaving us with hesitations, suspicions, angers, and hatred that have corroded our friendship with God."[44] There are other ways of saying this that may be closer to the mark:

For many the issue is not anger but numbness and indifference. A certain resignation seems to characterize many Western Christians. This may come to expression in the following sentiments: My work-a-day world is the real world that shapes and engages me, not my spiritual life; I have to get on with my life—God seems absent far too often; prayer seems to make little difference, so I have to take charge.

There are many other ways of expressing how many Western Christians feel spirituality bereft. They are like spiritual orphans in a world of productivity and technology.

Here, heart darkness is like a great fog. The tall buildings are still there, they just can't be seen. Similarly, God is with us by faith, and the spiritual world has impregnated our world of family, work, and culture, but we can no longer see. And over time, we don't care so much anymore whether we see or not. A spiritual malaise begins to permeate our very being.

Clearly one cannot escape secularism. Its influence is all around us. But one can always become more deeply grounded in God. In the practice of the spiritual disciplines, including the commitment to prayer, one may learn to dwell in and with God in ways that keep us centered.

With God as our dwelling place we can fully engage our world without being overcome or overwhelmed. And in this we need not only the breath of the Spirit upon us but also companions for a journey that will challenge us each step of the way.

The Crisis
Recognizing the depths to which we can sink

IN SOME CHRISTIAN CIRCLES THE LANGUAGE OF CRISIS is seldom heard. If God is good, the world is basically good, and if I am also okay, then the language of crisis is mere sensationalism. This is the lackluster position of a benign, liberal theology that knows little of the power of conversion and transformation.

But in more conservative, evangelical churches the language of crisis is also conspicuous by its absence. There is no need, so the thinking goes, to speak of crisis, because the great crisis has occurred; that is, one has come to faith in Christ through a dramatic conversion. There are no other crises to be had. Christ has won the victory over sin and death and the believer now shares in that victory.

Both groups have oversimplified the rich tapestry of the Christian experience. Coming to faith may be a crisis experience. It may also be a gradual awakening. But to presume that all is smooth sailing after one's conversion is to be blind to the history of Christian spirituality and to the testimony of many good women and men of faith.

Nouwen's voice can be a further testimony: "[E]verything came crashing down—my self-esteem, my energy to live and work, my sense of being loved, my hope for healing, my trust in God . . . everything."[45]

Those with a medical or psychological background may be quick to point out that this may simply be a general health or emotional breakdown. To some extent it is. But there is more to the story. This was a deeply personal crisis for Nouwen, which affected everything, including his life of faith. Besides his surprising insecurities and his constant need for affirmation and assurance, Nouwen's friendships and the crisis of his sexual identity brought his world to a near collapse.

Nouwen is hardly alone in such an experience. While the factors that precipitate such a crisis may vary, something may plunge us into heart darkness.

A crisis of health, relationship, vocation, identity, finance, or a major social crisis, may spill out in such a way that everything is affected, including one's relationship with God. Thus while a crisis may draw us to the Father's bosom, it may also repel us from God's gentle whispers. As a result, we may end up, not only depressed, but also blaming God for his failure of care and protection.

There are no easy solutions to this kind of spiritual crisis, this form of heart darkness, where like the setting sun in the tropics, darkness quickly descends upon a previously brightly lit landscape.

The way forward is not a sullen withdrawal or self-pity, but the cry of anger and the voice of lament. From the depths of my darkness, O Lord, I cry unto you. Let my voice reach your hearing. May you have pity on me and turn my darkness into light, my mourning into rejoicing, my brokenness into healing, my self-pity into the grace of your embrace.

A Fearful Stripping
Recognizing our need for further transformation

WHAT THEOLOGIANS CALMLY CALL SANCTIFICATION BY THE SPIRIT—the process of growth that follows justification by faith in Christ—is at the experiential level often a less than calm, gentle, and easy process. In fact, while some dimensions of sanctification may be like gentle falling rain, other aspects can be quite tumultuous, like a summer's tropical storm.

The basic movement of initial conversion has to do with the reparation of our relationship with God. But further conversions are also called for, and these involve not only our relationships with others, but also our relationship with ourselves.

Sanctification has to do with an inner spiritual growth where we grow in Christ-likeness and the fruits of the Spirit. This growth has to do with inner transformations, and one of the most startling has to do with the transformation of the kind of self we have constructed.

One form of heart darkness may have nothing to do with our relationship with God or with others, but may have everything to do with the way we view ourselves and the way we function as a consequence.

Henri Nouwen points out that many of us have created "the false self . . . fabricated . . . by social compulsion."[46] While this may be an over-simplification with regard to the complexity of who we are and who we are becoming, there is a key challenge in what

Nouwen is saying. The challenge revolves around the fact that our sense of self is often constructed more around the themes of reaction rather than around love. Moreover, our sense of identity is often formed more by the values of family and society than by the heartbeat of the gospel with its message of grace and forgiveness.

As a result, a fearful stripping process may need to take place. A confrontation with one's self needs to occur. This confrontation is not an act of violence. But it is an act of courage.

The movement of this confrontation, as part of the process of sanctification, is the recovery of the vision of who God intends us to be in Christ. Thus it is the re-formation of the self in the light of the grace of God and in the light of the gospel, which speaks of love, healing, and forgiveness.

The fearful self is invited to grow in trust in God and in relation to others. The compulsive self is invited to grow in the acceptance of the love of God as the core of life's meaning, thereby learning to transcend the fact that the self is valuable and acceptable only in terms of achievement and productivity.

There are many dinted selves that need to be re-crafted by the hand of the Great Ironsmith. But the most fundamental of all self-confrontations has to do with facing the hidden self, those illusive parts of ourselves that so much determine how we function.

The self is never healed by its own effort. It is a relational healing that needs to take place. We, therefore, are healed and made whole in the great love and generosity that God has for us and from whom we may hear the words: "You are my beloved daughter, my beloved son."

Rootless
Recognizing our need for commitment and community

THERE ARE MANY WAYS in which we may be plunged into heart darkness: An accident. An illness. A relationship breakdown. Loss of a loved one. A financial crisis. Usually when these sad things occur we at least know what we have to face.

But there are also far more subtle ways in which heart darkness can be compounded: A melancholic or fearful disposition. A family upbringing marred by negativity. A lackluster career. In these and others ways goodness in our lives is eroded, and the wellsprings of our inner being may be running on empty.

One of the ways in which a further erosion may occur has to do with some of the dominant values of our culture, the key of which is the notion of the autonomous self, exemplified in ideas of independence and self-sufficiency. To live this way is to cut ourselves off from the sources of life and to deny the basic movement of the entire biblical narrative.

Nouwen speaks about this within the framework of fear. Fear, he points out, can bind us to unhealthy routines, but it can also turn us "into wanderers who go from one place to another without direction or goals. Our emotions and feelings then become like a wild river that leaves the bed and destroys the land instead of irrigating it."[47]

It is not only fear that can turn us into wanderers. The adventurer can also be a wanderer, as can the person unskilled in developing meaningful relationships. But something much more fundamental is at play here. The very realities of our urban way of life, the job market, and the cultural values fostering narcissism all contribute to this fundamental sense of rootlessness.

That rootlessness contributes to heart darkness is more than self-evident, for the heart of our very being needs to be nurtured and cared for. The heart of who we are has to do with relationships of mutuality and trust. One cannot live well if one has no address and if no one is waiting and one is not known.

All of this speaks to the importance of community for heart wellness. Not any sort of community, however, will do. A community of faith cannot be a community merely for the purposes of receiving religious goods and services. A consumer Christianity does not build community and will never be able to.

A community of faith for heart wellness is a community of worship, teaching, and sacrament. It is also a community of relationships and place. It is a community where we are known and loved and where we receive and serve.

Such a community requires commitment to people, to mutual service, and to sharing life together. In this community Christ is the center, and life is lived together in gratitude, trust, and openness. In such a life there are companions on the journey.

Despite the models that we have from popular culture, to be alone and rootless is not a "cool" way to live. Such a life will narrow the arteries of one's inner being. Inner growth is growth with God and others in the community of life. This life-giving experience banishes the icy fingers of doubt and isolation that contract rather than expand the heart of love.

Absence
Recognizing the absent presence of God

WHETHER WE LIKE IT OR NOT, the Christian life cannot be lived and experienced with any sort of scientific certainty. It can be lived only in the beauty and pain of faith.

When we speak of faith we acknowledge that this is multi-dimensional. Faith has an object. It is faith in God through Christ. It is faith in the veracity of the biblical story's revealing who God is, who we are, the nature of the human condition, and the way in which God in his great love seeks us out and calls us to his forgiving heart.

But faith is also existential. I have faith. I live in faith and trust toward the God who has revealed himself in Scripture.

None of this, however, quite gets to the mystery that is faith. Faith is also a spiritual gift. It is born in us by the work of the Holy Spirit. And as such this faith is illuminating and reassuring.

The basic movement of faith has to do with presence. It is faith in the God who is there—the God who has created the world, who redeems his people, and who will one day fully make all things new and whole.

But faith also has to do with absence. It is faith in the God who has come and will come. It is faith in the God who has made himself known and who is shrouded in mystery.

Henri Nouwen once made the observation "that both presence and absence can deepen the bond of friendship."[48] He primarily had human relationships in view. But this may also be true in our journey of faith.

While it is possible that some people only ever have a very vague sense of God, as may be the case with many of us who say we believe in God but have nothing to do with a faith community or church and do not engage in any of the spiritual disciplines, the opposite may also be the case. People do have very key spiritual experiences. They have visions. They sense God's presence. They believe that God has spoken to them in some way.

What is particularly difficult for these people is coming to terms that this may not be the normal scheme of things. Visions may cease and God's presence may become woefully absent.

Many spiritual writers have spoken about this as the dark night of the soul, where God's consoling presence has turned into an experience of seeming desolation. And in this absence the Christian pilgrim is invited into a deeper walk of faith.

This form of heart darkness usually causes us to engage in deep introspection and frequent self-blame. We tend to think: God is displeased, and that is why the Great Lover has withdrawn.

But while some forms of heart darkness need to be resisted and overcome, the dark night needs to be embraced. This places us in a posture of waiting and emptiness. This is akin to a desert experience, a dreadful purgation.

While we may be tempted to protest or to solve the problem, the absent presence of God is a season in the spiritual journey that needs to be embraced. In this way the troubled heart becomes the waiting heart.

Lost
Recognizing our lack of centeredness

BEING LOST IS ONE OF THE MOST BASIC OF ALL HUMAN REALITIES and fears. It is archetypically woven into the very fabric of our being.

We have all had experiences of being lost. And we often wonder, at various junctures in our life's journey, whether we have lost our way. We are no longer sure whether what we are about is meaningful and purposeful.

Being lost at the theological level is like being lost in a wood or forest. What is scary about being lost in this way is being separated from parents or others who know the way. Thus lostness, theologically, is being separated from God and others. But there is more. While being lost in the woods need not mean that one has done something wrong, this is not the case in our relationship with God. Our separation is one of estrangement. The roots of our lostness lie in foolish reaction, unwillingness to listen, and a total reticence to obey.

Coming to faith is all about being found. It is homecoming. It is, in Christ, returning to be with God. This returning has everything to do with God's seeking activity, not only with our repentance.

This returning is not simply about some personal crisis. Its meaning lies much deeper. Coming to faith is a recovery of God's centrality in our lives. The God whom we neglected or ignored becomes the God whom we now love, worship, and obey.

But this initial and most fundamental of homecomings to the heart of God is not the only journey we need to make. Having come home, we can and do lose our way. This does not necessarily mean losing our faith but losing our life direction, which is meant to be centered in God.

Henri Nouwen, in an important transitional phase in his life writes, "I have the sense of being terribly busy without really feeling that I am moving down the right path."[49] We can write our own sub script to this key text: I feel in the midst of my much doing that I have lost all sense of God's presence; I am no longer sure that my present vocation is fulfilling the purposes of God; I am afraid that having once entered the house of faith I have now been living in the house of doubt.

All of this is to say that we can and do lose our way. We do so in our relationship with God and in relation to others, and vocationally and spiritually we can be in crisis.

Thus we need to be re-centered. And this is most basically a contemplative experience. In developing a new attentiveness to God in listening and in prayer we can begin to see more clearly the changes and adjustments we need to make.

Thus in one sense we need to be found again and again. And such is the God of the biblical story. Yahweh is the ever liberating and renewing God, and in the face of Christ and in the light of the Gospels this God ever seeks us, even when we are the most wayward.

This God also seeks to guide and direct us in life's decisions and choices. But for God's gentle voice to be heard we need to adopt a posture of humility and receptivity and grow a heart that loves to do the will of God.

Decay
Recognizing our ultimate finitude

THERE IS NO SINGLE MELODY LINE to the discordant music of heart darkness. Sometimes heart darkness is due to malevolent forces. Always it is related to the fundamental woundedness of the human condition and of our world. And many times it has to do with our own struggles, difficulties, waywardness, and foolishness.

But there is a most basic melody line. We can be gripped, disempowered, and overwhelmed by the fundamental movement of our existence to disintegration, decay, and death.

Nouwen rightly points out that "that's why we are so deeply affected by life's disappointments and setbacks. They remind us that sooner or later, everything decays."[50]

The recognition of our finitude and limitation begins early in our life's journey. In our childhood years we soon become aware that the whole world does not revolve around us, and that life is full of boundaries and limitations. While our adolescent years may be temporarily filled with our endless energy and seeming invincibility, the growth in further maturity is a bloodying experience. We suffer defeats and disappointments. We make mistakes. We hurt others and others hurt us.

The heart can darken around these painful realities. We may fail to come to terms with our limitations. We may find it difficult to accept the brokenness of our lives and world. We may find it hard to accept that everything that we do, including the good, does not always have a good outcome or may over time fall into decay. These things may harden the arteries of the heart.

So how do we respond to all this? Since denial is not the way forward, there is only one path we can take, and that is to embrace life's difficulties and our inherent vulnerability and the eventuality of our death.

While we in the West sometimes foolishly think that everything is possible and that we can change things for the better, unlike those in the Third World who more readily accept life's injustice, decay, and death, we do have to learn that everything is not possible. We can't stop aging, nor can we prevent decay in our relationships and institutions, including our churches. All is subject to the law of death.

But this is not the end of the story. We can commit ourselves into the hands of the God in Christ who tasted and embraced death and broke forth in new life. In the Christian faith the Resurrection is the story of good news.

This power of renewal, of resurrection, can be experienced in our broken relationships, in our vocational confusion, and in our institutional decay. And most finally, we may live in the hope of the renewal and healing of all things, our bodies as well as the nations.

Decay is real. So is renewal and healing. Death is a reality. But so is faith in the power of the Resurrection.

Eucharist
Recognizing sources of healing

THERE IS LITTLE DOUBT THAT OUR DOMINANT CULTURE, particularly in North America, is a culture of denial. We celebrate youth and can't face the realities of aging. We sentimentalize the idea of the nuclear family and can't acknowledge its demise and its brokenness. We laud the notion of the individual and can't see the desperate quest for community. We uphold the value of freedom but don't disclose how invasive authorities and institutions have become in our lives. And possibly worst of all, we continue to act as if the world revolves around us, and so we make sure it does by shaping economic realities that favor us.

This is the time when we need to acknowledge our heart darkness and our brokenness. This is also true of many of our churches, which have largely become culturally captive institutions. With our consumer Christianity, churches have begun to live a spiritual minimalism that knows little of a celebrative and obedient following of Jesus the suffering servant.

The time has come for us to acknowledge that the candle of God's overt presence has been removed and we are called into the desert for purgation and purification. The time is here for us to enter into the grieving heart of God.

Henri Nouwen reminds us that "in the breaking of the bread together, we reclaim our own broken condition rather than denying its reality." He continues, "We are broken, not in revenge or cruelty, but in order to become bread which can be given as food to others."[51]

This is indeed the place where we need to find ourselves again, or more accurately, the place where we need to be found. This place is the foot of the cross. This place is the Eucharistic table. This place is the place of contrition. It is also the place of lament.

The few centuries in which a triumphalistic Western world dominated much of the globe are still with us. But the days when an equally triumphalistic Western Christianity of cultural superiority spanned the globe are long gone. A new Western humility is called for, and the church in the West is called to repentance.

These larger configurations of heart darkness need healing as well as the personal dimensions of our lives. And so we need to come to that place where death speaks of life and where brokenness is the invitation to healing. That place brings us back to the Christ of Golgotha and to the table where broken people partake of broken bread as a sign and sacrament of the healing and new life that is offered to each one of us and offered to the whole world.

Heart darkness spilling its way into relational and community darkness need never be the final word. The God of the biblical narrative spoke light into being. He also gave his Son as light to the world to dispel the darkness in our lives and world. Darkness acknowledged becomes darkness dispelled, but a hidden darkness ever grows in its destructive power.

HEART
AND HAND

*Self-giving and Receiving
in the Midst of Loving and Serving*

IT IS POSSIBLE SERIOUSLY TO MISUNDERSTAND the writings of Henri Nouwen. Because Nouwen is so personal and so self-preoccupied with the issues of his life and the struggles of his faith, one may easily gain the impression that Nouwen's spirituality is only about one's interiority and self-development.

This reading of the author is to miscue. Yes, spirituality is about one's inner life. It does have to do with one's engagement with Scripture and the Eucharist. It is about one's participation in the community of faith. But this is by no means the whole picture.

The fact that there is more to the story sets Nouwen apart from much of the present-day interest in spirituality. Much of contemporary spirituality is primarily about self-interest. It is part of our culture's preoccupation with the therapeutic. So we do dieting, exercise, drug therapy or counseling, and self-development via certain spiritual practices. The goal, however, is not the formation and growth of the self in relation to the other or in relation to God. Instead, the orientation is toward personal wholeness as self-creation. Nouwen moves in a different direction in two important ways. The first is that growth in wholeness comes through the grace of God in Christ. Wholeness, therefore, is not an achievement but a blessing, a gift. And second, spirituality has to do with the whole Gestalt of one's life as it is oriented toward love of God and love of neighbor.

So, while much of contemporary spirituality has primarily the self in view, Nouwen's understanding of spirituality is profoundly relational, communal, and missional. It is particularly this last point that I wish to explore in this section.

Heart, head, and hand belong together. Theology, spirituality, and mission are linked. The deeds of the hand are formed in the head and motivated by the heart. Spirituality, therefore, has to do with the configuration of the whole of one's life, including a life of witness and service.

We see these contours throughout the writings of Henri Nouwen. What is so easily lost from view is that Nouwen was in every way an activist: priest, psychologist, educator, spiritual director, author, advocate on behalf of the world's poor, and pastoral worker with people with severe physical and intellectual disabilities. His life was not lived in holy isolation on some mountaintop. It was lived in the midst of a life of work and service.

As a result, Nouwen is a helpful guide for us who also live our lives in the midst of family, community, and work. He points us both to God as the source of life and to the neighbor as the one we are called to bless and serve.

Spirituality, therefore, always orients us in three directions at the same time: toward God, the self, and the other. Thus the healthy self is neither self-made nor self-preoccupied. It is centered in the goodness and love of God in Christ. And it is oriented outward to the other in a whole variety of ways.

A spirituality rooted in God is no narrow spirituality. It is a spirituality as wide and deep as the wisdom and goodness of God. It has in view the doing of all of God's good to others: the practical and the spiritual, the personal and the communal.

In essence, the hands that receive are the hands that give when the heart has been transformed from self-indulgence and self-focus to doing the love of God to all.

Prayer

The opening of heart and hand toward the other

PRAYER IS READILY STYLIZED AND REDUCED TO A FORMULA we use in our personal emergencies and in our church liturgies. That prayer is far richer is a promise waiting to be realized. And that prayer has both vertical as well as horizontal dimensions is a spacious place we need to inhabit.

Henri Nouwen opens up for us some of these wider spaces. He writes, "[W]hen you pray, you discover not only yourself and God, but also your neighbor. For in prayer, you profess not only that people are people and God is God, but also, that your neighbor is your sister or brother living alongside of you."[52]

That prayer can be a multifaceted form of discovery is not readily understood. We tend to think of prayer as an articulation of what we know and need.

But prayer can indeed open up the unknown, the unrecognized, and the hidden spaces in our lives. To the degree that prayer is a form of disarmament, a form of self-disclosure, and the impulse of the seeking heart, to that extent prayer can become revelatory and a powerful form of un-concealment.

In prayer a certain unveiling can take place. We may end up looking at the familiar with new eyes and in new ways.

What I am suggesting is that prayer leads to a new attentiveness. And this attentiveness can be and ought to be multidirectional.

There are many ways of expressing this. When I become more attentive to myself I may also become more attentive to others who affect me and whom I affect. Or conversely, if I become more aware of my neighbor for whom Christ died and for whom the full gift of life is intended, then I may also become more aware of myself and how I respond or fail to act toward my neighbor.

More primarily, my new attentiveness to God will make me more aware of both the gifts and goodness that God has given, and the areas of darkness and woundedness that persist in my life. However, the God of the Bible never draws attention only to me. Since God is a people-building God and the One who seeks the other, God will always turn my attention to others: family, friends, neighbors, colleagues, even enemies.

That the prayer of the heart directs my hand in loving witness and service to others gives service a profound spirituality. Service is not simply service. It is a sacramental activity.

In loving service to the neighbor we may become a sign and sacrament of the Reign of God for that person or that community. Service born out of prayer and prayerful service may open windows for people to see the loving heart of God.

While service is the doing of any good to the other, the movement of service is that the other may enter the wide spaces of the goodness of God. All Christian service while horizontally expressed is vertically motivated and oriented.

Prayer engages the neighbor. As such, it is a hidden work, the fruit of which is loving service.

Critical Engagement
The power of self-reflection and social engagement

MUCH OF THE THINKING AND WRITING ABOUT CHRISTIAN SPIRITUALITY may give the impression that this has to do with distancing and escaping from the real world rather than engaging it. Thus spirituality is seen as flight from the world and its evils.

A spirituality that seeks to escape the issues of our time is not a biblical spirituality, since the Bible reveals a God who engages the world for its salvation, liberation, and healing. But a biblical spirituality rightly emphasizes the value and importance of creating distance. It is here, in particular, that the metaphor of desert comes into play. One leaves the city to enter the desert for a season of reflection and purgation. But having been in the desert one returns to the city empowered with a new vision and zeal. Having been transformed in the desert one re-enters society with a transformational vision.

Nouwen puts all of this in other words: "[N]o mystic can prevent himself [or herself] from becoming a social critic, since in self-reflection he [or she] will discover the roots of a sick society."[53]

If one is simply immersed in the world, one will also be influenced by the world. And it is not very likely that one will be able to engage the world in creative and renewing ways.

In order to change the world one must first be inspired by a vision of new possibilities, and the beginning of this is to disengage and to create distance. However one does this is what we call entering the desert.

To enter the desert is to enter into a reflective place. It is a place of solitude and prayer. It is a place where one seeks the face of God and the wisdom and ways of God. This place may become the place of encounter. It may become a place of self-confrontation.

In exploring the contours of our own brokenness, woundedness, and waywardness we may begin to recognize the way in which these things are part of the wider dimensions of our society. This recognition is not so that we can excuse ourselves and blame the world. This is not to escape personal responsibility. But in the quest for our own personal resolution, healing, and renewal, this may open the windows for the healing of others and for finding new ways to bless our world.

Christian service to the world should always seek to affirm good and to transform what is evil. This evil in the world needs first to be recognized in ourselves. Then, in the light of that personal evil, we are first called to enter into God's healing ways. And so we become witnesses to the world, pointing to the God who seeks to make all things whole and new.

The challenge facing the church is not to engage the world on the world's terms. The church can only meaningfully engage the world when the church itself has gone through its own purgation and lives the grace of God's healing goodness.

The God Who Is There
Acknowledging the God who is ahead of us

IT IS EVER SO EASY TO DIVIDE THE WORLD UP into neat little categories: This is a good community. That is a bad one. This is the good empire. That is the evil one.

I have lived for over seven years in what was regarded as a bad neighborhood in East Vancouver, Canada. But in reality I have never lived in such a welcoming, culturally diverse, and life-giving part of the city. Everywhere in this neighborhood are the signs of goodness. And yes, there are many problems as well: poverty, high unemployment, lack of affordable housing. This list goes on and on.

The problem with neat categorizations is that they blur reality. In the good empire there is much evil and in bad neighborhoods there is much that speaks of community and care.

Henri Nouwen makes the helpful observation that "the Bible is a realistic book and does not avoid any part of human reality." He continues, "God is not only where it is peaceful and quiet, but also where there is persecution, struggle, division, and conflict."[54]

This reflection is particularly relevant when we think about a Christian's presence in the world. The Christian is called to inhabit not only the good places in our world as if God were only present there. Instead, we are called to inhabit the fearful and difficult places in our world, because God is also there.

The God of the biblical narrative is the God who is there. This God hears the cry of his people and delivers from captivity and oppression. This God has entered the human fray in Jesus Christ. This God has more fully entered the realities of our world than any other by taking upon himself the whole sinfulness and brokenness of humanity.

God is thus at the heart of the world. God is in the very depths of its need. As a result, the community of faith, through its members, can and should make itself present anywhere and everywhere: in the better suburbs and in the poorer neighborhoods; in multi national corporations and in small businesses; in state-funded schools and in private Christian colleges; in the media and in places of prayer; in the film industry and in refugee camps.

No place is of itself a sacred place. Every place can become a sacred place because of God's presence and the presence of those who love and serve in God's name. Thus a monastery can become such a sacred place. And so can a drop-in center in the midst of skid row.

We have a God who is there, and our calling is to see, to celebrate, and to join with God's overt or hidden action among us.

God is ahead of us God is at work in our world by his Spirit. The brooding and creative Spirit is the life-giving Spirit. God's Spirit is never restricted to the sanctuary. The Spirit hovers even over the places of degradation and fear. Thus even the desert may bloom.

Those who believe in this God and who seek to follow God's ways are invited to follow God in all the places of our world, the places of goodness and the fearful places.

Faithfulness
The contours of obedience and suffering

WHENEVER WE THINK OF CHRISTIAN SERVICE the person and work of Jesus Christ immediately come into view. We want our service to somehow reflect the life of Christ. We also want to be forgiving, healing, and life-giving members of our families and communities.

Unfortunately, the ministry of Jesus has not always been seen in a very integrated way. Some congregations seek only to emphasize Jesus' proclamation of good news. Others focus only on his acts of power such as healing and other charismatic gifts. Other congregations make Jesus' prophetic witness and resistance to the religious and political authorities of his day the main focus of his ministry.

Clearly the challenge is that we should embrace the Christ of the Gospels, not the Jesus of our own making. And we need to see every dimension of the life and witness of Jesus as relevant for our service in the world.

What this means is that we as individuals, and particularly as communities of faith, are to participate in all of the three "offices" of Christ as prophet, priest, and king. Therefore, proclamation, healing and other gifts, prophetic witness, care for the poor, and the work for justice are all part of our witness and service to the world.

This vision to embrace the whole Christ rather than the preferred Christ of our own making, means that we also need to embrace the possible consequences of following Christ in this way. As Nouwen has pointed out, "Jesus' life of faithful service did not end in a peaceful and tranquil death."[55] Nor, we may immediately add, did it consist of a peaceful life!

This opens up one of the great challenges of Christian service. We may not assume that obedience to the way of Christ and faithful service in his name will simply lead to goodness and blessing for all concerned. It may also lead to suffering.

In the biblical Anabaptist tradition, Christian service has to do with following the suffering Messiah into the world. Serving in the way of Christ will invite us into the cost of discipleship. Living, loving, and giving in the way of Christ may well call us into downward mobility and identification with the poor and marginalized.

Faithful service in the way of Christ is to become a peacemaker, reconciler, and healer. But it also involves prophetic witness that calls the principalities and powers to account and demonstrates a different way to the world's ways of power, dominance, and oppression.

But above all faithful service is the way of the heart. It is all about the love of God spilling over into love of neighbor, including strangers and enemies. This kind of service in the way of Christ is possible only when we are sustained by the Spirit of Christ animating and empowering us.

Sacramental Service
Giving the gift of identification and solidarity

SERVICE AND SPIRITUALITY ARE OFTEN SEPARATED. Thus heart and hand remain unconnected. It is, therefore, not surprising that the hand readily falls into inactivity. Activity that loses its motivational center or that is not animated by the brooding and life-giving presence of the Spirit soon falls silent.

Loving service in family or community, for friend or stranger, can so easily become a duty. And in time it may become a deadening burden. As a consequence, this kind of service will no longer bless the other and will undermine the giver's inner life. The result is people serving out of resentment. One feels aggrieved because one does not get back in return. One is not sufficiently appreciated, or the fruits of one's service are not apparent. This kind of service can deeply scar our relationship with God and do damage to our inner being.

One possible and radical way forward is to reconceptualize the whole idea of service. So often service is seen as the extra we must do and not as something intrinsic to our spirituality.

One of the clearest indicators of this kind of disconnection is that we have made worship and service two totally distinct realities. I am proposing that they should become joined. While worship is directed toward God and our service is directed toward people around us, the two movements ought to be interlinked.

Let's pursue this a little more closely. Worship is service we render to God. And service to our family, to our brothers and sisters in the community of faith, and to the neighbor or colleague, is a form of worship. In serving them we desire to bring glory to God and well-being to the other.

Henri Nouwen provides the following insight: "[W]henever I touch your broken heart [, O Jesus], I touch the hearts of your broken people, and whenever I touch the hearts of your broken people, I touch your heart."[56]

These are important connections that Nouwen is making. According to this formula, there is a direct correlation between my orientation toward God and my care for others.

There is no stronger way to put all of this than in the words of Matthew's Gospel, chapter twenty-five: "Truly I tell you, just as you did it to one of the least of these who are members of my family, you did it to me" (v. 40).

Service, therefore, whatever form it may take, can carry the sacramentality of foot-washing. More broadly speaking, service is washing the feet of the world. Or to put that differently, loving service is baptizing the neighbor in the love of God. Or using the language of the Eucharist, service and care are both a physical and a spiritual giving of bread to the stranger and the needy.

Service inbred in the love of God and impregnated by the Spirit is sacramental. It carries with it the hidden seeds of the Kingdom of God, giving life to both the giver and the receiver.

Sowing in Faith
Entrusting our witness and service to God's care

WITNESS AND SERVICE ARE EXPRESSED IN A MYRIAD OF WAYS. Most fundamentally, these come to expression in the places we inhabit and among the people we regularly meet. Thus, our witness and service are incarnational and contextual. We don't witness to some abstract person "out there." Witness and service can take shape only in the midst of relationships in the home, community, church, and workplace, and in all the other ways in which we make social contact with others.

Much of our witness and service is incidental to what we are already doing. It is part of life's daily realities. Some of our service and witness may come from a greater intentionality when we are particularly seeking to bless someone or seek to contribute to a situation.

But whether spontaneous or intentional, our attempts to do something of God's good to others must come from a visionary place. Nouwen expresses this as follows: "[I]f a word is to bear fruit, it must be spoken from the future world into the present world."[57]

Nouwen's helpful insight can be elaborated upon. Our seeking to bless others must come from the place of love and the place of prayer. It is action in hope. It is serving in faith. It is doing what we can do in the expectation of the greater things that God alone can do.

Much of our serving is fundamentally anticipatory. It is seed for a good harvest. It is a small beginning for greater things to come.

Service, therefore, comes from an eschatological vision. It has in view the breaking in of God's kingdom. It looks for the activity of God's life-giving and renewing Spirit.

Service is not anything and everything that we do. Much of what we do is simply for ourselves or for our own. Christian service is for Christ and for the other. It has in view our joining with God in His purposes of forgiveness, healing, and transformation.

As a consequence, this form of service is always a form of humility and surrender. This is not us doing *our* thing. This is not our do-gooderism. This is not our needing to be needed. This is not a subtle form of control. This has to do with our giving our life away for the benefit and blessing of the other. Service and obedience and sacrifice are, therefore, closely linked.

Service first involves listening, not doing. It has to do with listening to God, to the Spirit, to the heart cry of others, and to one's own responsive heart. It may also involve listening to the wisdom of others before one acts. And in this listening to others we may well seek to draw others in so that our service becomes a communal activity.

But service is always a form of sacrifice. To say yes to the other means that we frequently have to say no to ourselves. And in saying yes to the other in loving service we first have had to say yes to God, seeking in prayer God's will and God's way for the person or situation.

Service is not mere activity. It is the movement of faith. It is sowing in hope. It is acting in prayer.

In the Midst of Doing
Losing our way in the midst of service

OURS IS A BUSY AND FRENETIC AGE. This is both surprising and not so. It is surprising in the light of all of the promises that have been made to us in the modern world: promises of easier working conditions due to the use of technology, more time for leisure, and more time for the pursuits of one's interests. That this is not so is due to the very nature of contemporary living, which has created a dominant culture that teaches us to be restless, demanding, and ever questing for the impossible dream of happiness framed by acquisition.

So, we are always terribly busy with ourselves, our family, and our work. And this busyness is both in terms of what we are actually doing and what we are ever thinking about.

Where, then, does Christian service fit into this picture? Do we simply add service to the church or to the neighborhood onto an already full personal agenda?

As if his teaching, writing, mentoring, and other aspects of his vocation were not enough to keep him busy, Henri Nouwen spent much of his adult life actively involved for social justice in Latin America. He writes, "[T]he long years of university teaching and the intense involvement in South and Central American affairs have left me quite lost."[58] What made him feel this way? Nouwen's lostness came from both over-busyness and a crisis regarding his vocational direction. One can't do everything.

Many of us can identify with Nouwen's experiences. I certainly can. Teaching, involvement in urban mission, and work in some of the poorer countries in Asia have kept me more than busy. Too busy, in fact!

This kind of busyness can hardly be regarded as a virtue. It is better seen as a problem, and it is indicative of our personality, our driven age, and a faulty theology. As a result, we lose ourselves in the midst of our doing.

That theology plays a part in our commitment to busyness needs to be accented. Despite the emphasis on grace in the evangelical tradition, sheer activism seems to be the order of the day. We need to care for our families, serve the church, do our jobs well, reach out to our neighbors, commit ourselves to the concerns of the Third World—and the list goes on.

But theologically speaking, there are several moves that need to be made in order to break us free from these rounds of demand. The first is that all of life is to be lived to the glory of God. Therefore, family is also service, and work can be mission.

Second, we are called to Sabbath, and this includes finding rest and refreshment in the midst of doing. It does not only mean setting a day aside for worship.

Third, our doing cannot be sustained by our own drivenness. The work of service is us playing our part, using our gifts *and* being sustained by the Spirit's power.

And finally, the greater challenge is to live in more integrated ways so that our life, work, and leisure become our mission.

Resistance
Saying "no" to the worldliness of the world

MISSION IS ALL ABOUT ENGAGING THE WORLD. Essentially it is entering the world with the love of God. At its heart, mission is doing all of God's good to others; it is spawned by grace, it is framed by compassion, and it seeks the *shalom* and well-being of the whole person in all of his or her relationships and in the context of that person's life.

But this is not the whole story. There is another side. Mission is not only about engagement; it is also about resistance.

Nouwen once made the helpful comment, "I am sent into the world; my friends have to help me not to become a part of it."[59] This comment needs careful elucidation. Whether Christian, agnostic, Muslim, Hindu, or Buddhist, we all live in the world and partake of its goodness. What Nouwen is referring to when he speaks of resistance is not in relation to the goodness of the world but to its worldliness.

Within a Christian framework, worldliness means in particular humanity's resistance and rejection of the ways of God. Worldliness at its heart has to do with the creation of and the worship of values and ideas that are counter to the gospel of forgiveness, healing, and reconciliation in Christ.

In the biblical story, worldliness has to do with the de-centering of God and the centering of our community or ourselves. And in this we see the politics of idolatry.

The follower of Christ, on the other hand, is called to a profound engagement with the world. As a sign of and a witness to the incarnational presence of Christ, the Christian is called to embed herself or himself into the social realities of our world. In every sphere of life Christians seek to be a blessing to others.

The obvious risk in this way of living life in the world is that one may become part of the problem rather than being the bearer of the life and love of God. Thus the messenger becomes sidetracked. The witness becomes blurred.

That this can readily happen is due to several key factors. First, the disciple of Christ is never without faults, weaknesses, and sins. Second, the Christian may cease to rely on the grace of God and the empowerment of the Spirit. And finally, the follower of Christ may become subject to seduction because of a lack of companions on the journey of faith and service.

The Christian life is to be lived *with* others. And Christian service is to be done *with* the support, prayers, and encouragement of the sisters and brothers in the community of faith.

In this common journey, which includes our embeddedness in the world as those who pray and serve, we need not only encouragement but also protection and care. And even more basically we may well need correction and redirection.

The joining of head, heart, and hand in the love of God and in the service of others, is always a rhythm of receiving and giving and giving and receiving. We receive God's love, grace, and forgiveness and extend goodness to others. But in giving we receive, in blessing we are blessed, in serving we are enriched.

Mediation
Being a window and gateway for the other

BEING A SERVANT OF CHRIST TO OTHERS will always involve us in conversation with others, since there are things to be shared. Our service to the world has to do with speaking about the good news of God in Christ.

But this talk is never to be the talk of idealism. It can only be the speech of faith. The difference between the two is crucial and critical.

The talk of idealism, while it may appear to be helpful, is ultimately destructive. This kind of talk attempts to put the best spin on anything and everything. It speaks of unhindered possibilities. It speaks of other worlds that are ours for the taking.

In the final analysis, this kind of talk, while seemingly encouraging, hopeful, and life-giving puts us on a quest of grasping the wind. It provides promises without an address. And this means finally that one is thrown back on one's own resources.

The language of faith is different. It is not vacuous. It is speech that bears witness to the experiential appropriation of the biblical story. The language says this: The God of which this ancient book speaks, is the God I have encountered and know personally.

This does not make my experience a source of hope for another person. The hope lies in the God of the biblical narrative. This hope is that the God who was freeing, gracious, and life-giving to his ancient people will also show his face of kindness and healing to my spouse, colleague, friend, neighbor, even my enemy.

Thus my witness is not the source of hope, but my testimony can be a form of corroboration. In essence what I am saying is that the God who has revealed himself in Christ to me is the God who also seeks to be gracious to you. And so, in one sense, we do mediate something. We can become a window or a gateway of hope for the other person.

While we may be tempted to think that we are this window when we are strong and confident, we may in fact be fooling ourselves. The way of God in the world is not so much one as triumphant king but as the suffering one. The way of God is the way of the cross.

Thus our best service and witness may, therefore, come from places of weakness. Nouwen suggests that we are "to help each other in making our brokenness into the gateway to joy."[60]

While God may wish to use our strength, resources, abilities, and enthusiasm, God may well use our brokenness and our empty hands. Thus what we mediate to others is not so much what we have, but what God can give.

To mediate well is not to point people to ourselves: We are not the saviors of the world but mere participants in the grace of God. Rather, it is to point people in the right direction and to testify that one has walked this road oneself.

We are therefore called to say a small yes to God's big yes to all who seek the path of life that leads to God's embrace in love and to a generous banqueting table.

In the Heart of the World
Seeing the God who is with us and among us

HENRI NOUWEN SAYS, "Our call to compassion is not a call to try to find God in the heart of the world, but to find the world in the heart of God."[61]

There are many ways that one could respond to this insight. The most basic is that for the Christian, living with compassion toward others has everything to do with finding, knowing, and responding to the heart of God.

There are fundamental reasons why this is so. A Christian is primarily a person who has been touched by the love of God. This love has been so healing and transforming that it becomes the heart out of which we live and serve. So we are compassionate because we are deeply loved in the very heart of God. And the way God loves us becomes the way in which we seek to reach out to others.

The rest of Nouwen's insight, which is cast in either/or terms, would be better framed in both/and categories. One can find God in the heart of the world and one can find the world in the heart of God.

It seems to me that the latter is always the move we should make first. In turning to God in worship, prayer, and solitude we will discover the heartbeat of God for the world—a world God called into being, a world he sustains, and a world that God is redeeming in Christ and renewing by his Spirit. The contemplation of God will unfold to us God's aching and healing heart for the world. Thus spirituality will always draw us back again into the issues of our time and the realities of our world.

The world that one finds in the heart of God is no ideal world. It is the world in all of its beauty and chaos, all of its winsomeness and despair. But it is a broken world wrapped in birth cloths of forgiveness and hope.

Furthermore, the world in the heart of God is not a partial world. It is not simply the world of the great and the powerful, and it's not a particular country or nationality. It is the whole world, and especially the world of the least and the little ones.

Seeing the world in the heart of God helps us to see God in the heart of the world. God is not simply "up there." And God is certainly not distant and removed. God upholds the world and constantly seeks to renew it.

Thus one can find God in the world: in places of power and in the streets of degradation, in major corporations and in families, in churches and in our communities. But God is not necessarily in all of these places in the same way. In places of power God may be with those who in humility seek to use power for the greater good of all. In the streets of despair God's healing presence may be with those crying for restoration.

But in whatever way God by the Spirit is at work in the world, God's presence is always a hidden presence. It is a presence possibly felt by all but understood only in faith.

Seeing God in the heart of the world gives our witness and service to the world a particular joy, for it is a re-seeing of the Beloved One. The One we see in prayer is also the One we may see in the workplace.

THE HEART'S TRUE HOME

Anticipating and Seeking God's Final Future

As you the reader have been making your way through these various reflections and have followed the structure of this book, you will have noted a certain order. We moved from recognizing the realities of the human condition to acknowledging our need for healing and wholeness in the love and grace of God.

We then went on to reflect on the need for the transformation of the heart to be supported by the renewal of our minds, and the further recognition that in the journey of faith we need companions on the way. Hence the call to friendship and community.

That we struggle and experience difficulties in this life of faith is a fundamental given. And we err badly if the life of faith is cast only in triumphal terms and not equally in terms of the seasons of doubt and the dark night of the soul.

Rather than destroying our life of witness and service, these struggles and difficulties give our mission a grace-filled humility. Our service to the world, in the way of Christ, is service in and through community and in a humility that acknowledges our own need for further growth in the goodness of God, the life of Christ, and the creativity of the Spirit.

However, our life both in community and in the workplace is always to be framed in and energized by hope. We live, work, and serve in the light of God's final future. Thus while responding to the present, we live in faith for the fuller in-breaking of the Reign of God.

This is important in several ways. Being God's eschatological people means that our final dreams and values do not lie here. We look for a world to come. This means that this world does not have the final say for our lives, but rather what God will yet do in the restoration of all things.

The further importance of this is that we, therefore, do not expect the world to give us what finally it cannot. The world sustains us physically and socially. It cannot give us eternal life. Relationships can give us support and encouragement, but they cannot make us whole. The products of our technological prowess can make life easier, but they cannot give us ultimate meaning.

The heart's true home is a resting place in the heart of God. This home is a home of longings, since we look for beauty, wholeness, and well-being. But this well-being is to be framed in the present presence of God and in the future when God will be all in all.

Homecoming here will always be partial, for we are still on pilgrimage. We are on the road to wholeness in Christ and life in the Spirit. The final arrival is not of our own making. It lies beyond us, beckoning. It calls us forward in anticipation and hope.

While this life is no rehearsal for the life to come, in that this is the life God has called us to live, this life is not the final act. There is more to the play of life. There is a grand finale, but this does lie in the history *we* are making. It lies in the consummation of God's final mending and healing of all things: Heaven and earth made one. Body and soul fully restored. All things made new in the newness of God.

Far from Home
Finding the center of our existence

WHETHER OR NOT WE LIKE TO HEAR IT we do have to acknowledge that what characterizes the human condition is a fundamental and devastating sense of loss. And while we may attempt to circumnavigate this troubling reality, it will always in the end lay us bare. No amount of relationships, things, and preoccupations can stave off the existential anxiety that is but one symptom of our lostness.

Within a Christian worldview, lostness is a relational reality. Lost from God, we become lost within ourselves, in our relationship with others and in relation to the created order.

Lostness is expressed in alienation. This alienation characterizes the social condition but also our relationship to the natural world.

Henri Nouwen observes that we are so "far from home that we eventually forget our true address." He continues: "Jesus does not speak about a change of activities or even a change of place. He speaks about a change of heart."[62] This notion gives our lostness a tragic poignancy. We may know that we are lost. But we no longer know how far we have wandered, how far we are from home and from God's intention for our lives.

Not knowing our true home means that we become part of the never-ending quest to make a true home for ourselves. This plays itself out on both the macro as well as the micro level.

Our society is rather quick to tell us what our true home is: a particular political ideology providing the frame for the pursuit of happiness, security, and the doubtful wonderment of much-having.

At the personal level we may set our own specific goals for home-coming: a good job or a good retirement; a home in the suburbs or the freedom of renting; marriage or the scope of uncommitted relationships. We all have our own ideas about the good life and the hope, meaning, and purpose we will find in it.

But however good all or some of the above may be, these are but the partial stopping places along the way. The heart's true home is the resolution of the spiritual quest. Homecoming is not so much about place, it is about relationship. And the greatest relationship is to know that one is known and loved by God in Christ.

This being known and loved feeds the inner quest and satisfies the inner longings of the human being to the point of final resolution. It is possible to confess: I have come home in knowing Christ and being known by him in the Spirit. And this homecoming provides the center, the wellspring, the inspirational core out of which one lives.

This homecoming is for this life and for the life to come. Qualitatively the same, the life in Christ by the Spirit lived here is also the life we will live across the awesome abyss. Thus we may speak of homecoming and a final and fuller homecoming, which is fundamentally the same, for it is the fuller unveiling, entering into the same life of God.

Having Seen
The promise of a hope and a future

WHILE IT IS ONLY TOO POSSIBLE TO LIVE WITH SADNESS and loss of hope, feeling the swirling edges of despair as they erode the sinews of life, it is still true that we all have a future. For some the future is dark. Others continue to live in hope.

To live the future in and of itself seems to be a most precarious endeavor. How uncertain and unpredictable the future seems to be: It lies beyond us. It is at the outer edges of our control. It comes to us unbidden and unannounced.

It comes as no surprise, therefore, that for some the future is colored by fear, while for others, the future is textured differently. It is a stranger to be welcomed rather than an enemy to be resisted.

What is critically important in this more positive approach to the future is the shaping of our past and the bridges we build into the future. Looking at our past first, we can note that the goodness of the past can carry us forward with hope into the future.

Nouwen writes, "I no longer can live without being reminded of the glimpse of God's graciousness that I saw in my solitude, of the ray of light that broke through my darkness, or the gentle voice that spoke in my silence."[63]

He is saying that the good and comforting presence of God in past times of reflection and prayer provides a basis for trust in the continued presence of God in the present and future. This central motif can be seen in many areas of life. A friendship rooted in the long journey of the past has promise for a future. The quality, integrity, and goodness of an institution provide the base for what it may and can be in the years and decades ahead. And this is how we live much of our lives: the goodness of the past as precursor of the goodness of the future.

But none of this is guaranteed. Things may go wrong. Thus the goodness of the past is only a *promise* of what the future may bring.

In the biblical story, however, the connection between past and future is not simply rooted in human precariousness. It is grounded in the nature and faithfulness of God. God is the God of the past and the future, and the nature of God is one of steadfastness and covenant faithfulness. Thus, God is the bridge between past and future. The uncertainty of the future need not be the abyss into which we fall in an anticipatory way.

Having seen, having believed, having tasted, having trusted, and having committed our lives into the tender care and life-sustaining goodness of Christ, we find that our future lies secure in the grace of God. We are being carried by the flapping wings of the Spirit who spans the ages.

This does not mean that nothing difficult will befall us. It most likely will. But even so, your hand, my God, will uphold me. Even in the darkest place I am not hidden from you. And in the changing circumstances that the future may bring, you will hold me fast. You, my God, are the One to whom I cling as I edge toward a future yet unknown.

Rooted

Finding home in the precariousness of prayer

THE SEARCH FOR HOME AND THE ATTEMPTS TO BUILD HOME are for many people the politics of safety and security. In a precarious world, safety has become a critical issue for many of us.

To build a home as a place of security is a complex undertaking, for to build such a home involves much more than having a house. It also involves a safe environment. It also has to do with resources in order to sustain a lifestyle. And finally, it has to do with being able to live certain values such as community peacefulness, celebration, and joy. Ultimately it has to do with relationships.

In many ways "home" is an idealization. It is a dream. It is an expression of an archetypal desire and need for a final place of belonging. It is here that one is truly known.

That we look for such a place is a manifestation of our humanity. We feel the need to belong, to be rooted, to be in solidarity, to be in community. And so we strive to find a place and to make such a place. Usually we seek to make such a place with others: with spouse, partner, friends.

This is a most appropriate human quest. That it may elude us is part of human fragility and vulnerability. Houses don't necessarily become homes. Relationships may break down. Community is difficult to build and maintain.

That home and homecoming is something more than we can build and achieve is evident in the human quest for meaning, ultimacy, intimacy, peace, and solidarity. As a consequence, we cannot fully find "home" at home. "Home" has to be found in the deeper caverns of an interior life. When found, home becomes an expression of the deeper rootedness that we have entered into.

Henri Nouwen's observations about prayer speak to these desires in us. He notes, "[C]ontemplative prayer keeps us home, rooted and safe, even when we are on the road."[64] What he is pointing to is that certain forms of prayer are a form of homecoming in the more ultimate sense of that word.

And so it is! Home is first and foremost an existence, a condition before it is a place. Therefore, homecoming is presence; it is a welcome to the heart of God. And prayer is the indwelling of that homecoming.

This homecoming to God in Christ through the Spirit is the heart's true home. This rootedness in God in faith and nurtured in a life of prayer is the final homecoming that partially comes to expression here. And so we form relationships. We build family. We gather in communities of faith. We create networks of association. We build and maintain institutions.

We don't build all of these because we are trying to find—rather, we have been found in Christ, and so we build these various ways of life together. These become a small foretaste of the great homecoming of humanity in the final *shalom* of God and the healing of the nations.

Pulling Us Forward
Responding to the movement of God's grace

LIVING THE CHRISTIAN LIFE IS TO LIVE ESCHATOLOGICALLY. Not only is it living toward a certain future in which the mending of the creation and the restoration of all things will take place, but also it is living the now differently.

This difference is the vision to live beyond the now in the now.

It goes without saying that living the Christian life should not be cast in escapist terms. It is about engaging the world because one has engaged the God of the Bible who is both creator of all that is and the great healer and restorer of all things.

Because God is the great restorer we are invited both to experience this restorative activity and to participate in the blessing and goodness that God ever seeks to bestow. As such, we live beyond ourselves. And we live beyond what appears to be humanly possible.

Henri Nouwen writes of the way in which God draws us forward: "It is not easy to let God's mercy speak to us because it is a voice asking for an always open relationship, one in which sins are acknowledged, forgiveness received, and love renewed."[65] Put differently, whenever we respond to God in faith and humility, God transforms us, pulls us forward, deepens us in his grace, and draws us into his purposes.

When we come to God in confession not only may we receive forgiveness but also we are invited into the healing purposes of God where we are empowered to sin no more in that and the other dimensions of our lives. Moreover, receiving forgiveness opens the door to forgive and bless others.

In whatever way we come seeking God we find more than we expected. And with the renewal of our inner being and the transformation of our minds we come to see more fully the audacious purposes God has for our world.

We begin to see that forgiveness does make a difference; that reconciliation between enemies is possible; that peacemaking rather than warmongering is a viable option in our world; that restitution is a powerful healer and transformer of persons and communities that have been harmed, neglected, or marginalized.

The person or group who is in any way touched by the grace and goodness of the living God is pulled forward into a larger vision of life. This gospel vision of peace with God and with others, and of the healing and restoration of all things, is a vision that both entices us and makes us aware of our frailty and limitations.

And so, living the vision beyond the now in the now invites us into the places of prayer, fasting, waiting. It invites us to cry, to lament, and to intercede. It empowers us to live for the one and only worthwhile thing: to see the in breaking of the Kingdom of God and God's healing spring up like the dawn.

Pushing the Boundaries
Living prophetic lives

THERE IS A SIMPLE BUT PROFOUND LOGIC that lies at the heart of the gospel. It is this: Living the grace of Christ in the power of the Spirit frees us from the death-dealing powers of our age in order to pursue the life-giving powers of the Reign of God. Put somewhat differently, the power of the love of God in Christ frees us not only from our own negativity, foolishness, and sin but frees us *for* the purposes of God. Thus called away from our own petty preoccupations we are invited into the wider spaces of God's renewing work.

Much of contemporary Christianity fails to understand this. Our focus is so often primarily on what God can do for me. There is a failure to grasp the idea that the greater freedom does not lie in my being free from my own waywardness and compulsions, but in being caught up in the vast purposes of the life-giving Spirit.

To live in the vast purposes of the Spirit is to live both eschato-logically and ecstatically. It is to be caught up in something much greater than ourselves and to live that something greater with passion and enthusiasm.

This passion can go in several directions at the same time. It can be expressed in relationship with God. Thus worship, prayer, contemplation, visions, and dreams become more a part of our religious experience rather than the dullness of heart that so frequently is our experience. Passion in the power of the Spirit and being graced with the charisms of the Spirit become the diet of our spirituality.

But this passion and ecstasy also needs to be worked out in relation to the world. Nouwen suggests that "those who live ecstatic lives are always moving away from rigidly fixed situations and exploring new, unmapped dimensions of reality."[66] And so it may well be, but ecstasy is visionary first, before it becomes part of our purpose in the world.

In the Spirit, the ground for living ecstatically is seeing what is possible: what God can and will do. And in the light of these visionary dimensions, the Christian can then live and act courageously and prophetically. Such a person is willing to take the risk of faith and count the cost of discipleship. Thus we challenge our own values. We change the priorities of our lifestyle. We live in repentance and in the Spirit and order our lives to the purposes of God in bringing hope and healing.

For the young this may sound like the ultimate adventure. For those of more conservative temperament this may sound like religious fanaticism. In reality it is neither. This is living in the way of Christ. It is the way of the cross. It is a form of self-abandonment into the hands and heart of God for our world.

Living prophetically and pushing the boundaries is for those who have hidden their lives in God and are not afraid, in the power of the Spirit, to be God's disturbing and transforming servants in the world.

Out of Fragility
Living hope in great humility

SINCE THE LIFE IN AND WITH GOD THROUGH THE SPIRIT is the heart's true home, then God is our hope, our certainty, our purpose, and our future.

This does not in any way mean that God is, therefore, on our side. Being with God does not mean that God is for us in the sense that God backs our wishes, programs, and ideologies. Sadly, some contemporary Christians seem to think that they have God in their back pockets.

Believing in God is not an invitation to the path of triumphalism. It all is so very different. It is a calling to a life of surrender and humility.

Thus God is not on *our* side. Rather we are called to the side of God, called to worship, prayer, obedience, and service. We are called to the way of God in the world, a way revealed in Christ, as the new way of forgiveness, suffering, humility, and self-giving love.

Therefore we live the certainty of faith in God and the assurance that the ways of God are the ways of life and empowerment, not as arrogant knowers of the truth, not as seeking to impose on others, not as those driven by religious ideology. Rather we live the certainty of faith in the cries and whispers of the heart that seeks a fuller manifestation of the Kingdom of God and the outpouring of the Spirit.

Henri Nouwen not only focuses on living the life of faith in greater humility, but also acknowledges our fundamental fragility. He notes "that it is possible to live the wounds of the past not as gaping abysses that cannot be filled and therefore keep threatening us, but as gateways to new life."[67]

Recognizing that we are merely sinners saved by the grace of Christ, the people of faith on a journey toward wholeness, those who ever seek to know God more fully and those who are ever challenged to live the gospel with greater faithfulness and integrity, we find that this gives our lives a particular texture. And so it is all about the life of love sculpted in vulnerability.

And so we can find "home" with others. We can be compassionate with the hurting, in solidarity with those who struggle for goodness and wholeness and in partnership with the poor. We can be at home with those who seek to resist the powers of this age.

The heart's true home is never a heart of isolation. It is not the self-guarded and self-protected heart. It is the heart with and in God that finds home with others whether they are the most powerful or the most needy.

Finding home with others is to love and serve them well. This is done most basically in the hope that goodness will come to them and that they too may find the heart's true home. This will always be their own discovery due to the brooding, enlightening, and life-giving Spirit.

Cries of the Heart
Finding a new voice of prayer

THE CHRISTIAN LIVES LIFE IN AN ANTICIPATORY WAY. He or she looks to the great mending of all creation and all things, but is nevertheless situated in all the realities of daily life and the issues of our time.

Christians are a colony of the age to come. They are resident aliens. They are too late for this world and too early for heaven.

Seen from a theological perspective, the people of God live in between the times. They have experienced the grace of Christ, the coming of the Spirit, and the in-breaking of the Reign of God. But they live in the hope of the fuller coming of the Kingdom of God when Christ will be all in all and all is renewed.

To live in this in-between space is a huge challenge. The vision of the life to come can so easily fade. The realities of our day-to-day existence can so easily overwhelm us. Thus to be God's resident aliens will always be a life of struggle and prayer.

Living as a colony of the age to come is to live in both joy and pain. Joy is the fruit of having come home to the loving heart of God. But pain is the reality of our existence living in a broken world, being far from whole ourselves, and seeing the ongoing suffering of our world.

Thus what characterizes us, as those living between the times, are cries from the heart. Nouwen reminds us that "to pray is to unite ourselves with Jesus and lift up the whole world through him to God in a cry for forgiveness, reconciliation, healing, and mercy."[68]

This expansive union and concern shows something of the width and depth of Nouwen's compassion. My cries of the heart are often more limited. While there are times when I groan about the beauty and brokenness of our world, the ongoing march of injustice, the plight of the poor, and the persistence of oppression, often my vision is narrower. My cries of the heart are for a particular person, a community, people that I associate with, places where I work.

That we have different capacities in carrying the burdens of our world is stating the obvious, but that we are the burden bearers of our world lies at the heart of the gospel. In following Christ, who gave his life for the world, we thereby are called to a similar service. And while love is central and witness is important and service is the practical outworking, our giving of our lives for the world also has to do with prayer.

There is much to cry about. There is much to lament. There is also much goodness in our world, but so much of that goodness is for the few rather than for the many.

In the heart of God the whole world finds a place, including the world of the excluded ones. In our hearts, ever self-protecting, greater spaces need to be created. Space for spouse, children, and friends needs to be made. But space for the neighbor, the political refugee, the poor also needs to be forged if we are to carry the whole world in prayer to the loving and healing heart of God.

Emptiness
Creating open places for the Spirit

LIVING AS THOSE ANTICIPATING THE AGE TO COME when the presence and glory of God will be all in all does not mean that we are full of the present and the future. Fullness belongs to God, and for us there are the gifts of God's love and goodness, and there are the struggles, and the need for empty spaces.

To be full of the purposes of God and to be filled with the Spirit and to be full of the future hope that awaits us does not mean that all is well with us, all is under control, and all is taken care of.

We live all of this in faith. We look to this God who is ahead of us. We are not the possessors of these things but the grateful recipients of all that God continues to give.

Therefore, living eschatologically is not living confidently, or fearfully, but living prayerfully. And at the heart of this posture of prayerfulness lies the wisdom not only to speak but also to listen, not only to act but also to wait.

Nouwen suggests that "every relationship carries within its center a holy vacancy, a space that is for the first love, God alone."[69]

But, creating empty spaces is not what our present-day culture does well. We don't have much practice at it. More often, we do the opposite. Fullness is what we are promised: a life full of working and playing, and filled with having and acquiring. This kind of life, our culture tells us, will give us the happiness and fulfillment we seek.

The church often does not help us at this point, either. It is full of religious activity: worship, teaching, fellowship, service. The busy round of religious activities is added to the secular demands of our ever-busy lives.

The call to live eschatologically, anticipating God's final future, is no drumbeat to march conquering into the world as those with all the answers for humanity. Those hoping for God's future are not the crusaders of this world. They are the waiters. They wait on God. They wait to listen. They wait to see the stirring of the waters. They wait for the leading of the Spirit. They wait for the visions of God.

Out of this waiting comes another form of being waiters. Having waited on the call of God they can now wait on tables that serve the feast of God. They can carry the bread and wine of God to a needy world.

To wait for God is a holy activity. It is eschatological in nature, for it anticipates the God who will come.

No one who is full waits. The one who is full acts out of this fullness. But the one who is empty waits. And at the core of our being, fullness should not be a major key. Emptiness should be. A holy waiting is living eschatologically.

We are afraid of such empty spaces. We are comfortable with fullness, never mind what we are full of as long as we are full. But empty spaces remind us of our humanity, our limitations, our fragility. It is these spaces that become the places of prayer, worship, and true attentiveness. In the empty place we can be filled with the fullness of God.

From Beyond
Open to the Supernatural

WHATEVER WE MAY THINK of the philosophical and ethical contours of late modernity, and whatever we may think of the revival of interest in spirituality in the last two decades, the overwhelming worldview that still dominates us is an undiluted pragmatism. Ours continues to be an age of rationalism and utilitarianism.

Our profound preoccupation is with the world of our own making. And more specifically, we are engrossed with our own small world of living, loving, studying, working, relaxing, achieving, and producing.

That we are significantly this-worldly oriented is stating the obvious. That we are obstinately preoccupied with ourselves is a confession we all need to make.

While much in our world is marked by goodness, living this pragmatism and self-interest is finally not life-giving. However scandalous it may seem, we need to be saved from ourselves, a notion we find affronting, considering that we see ourselves as *so* self-sufficient!

This idea of needing to be saved has to do not only with our sinfulness and waywardness but also with our preoccupations. And much of these preoccupations have to do with the major values of our culture, where the dollar is so often the bottom line, and human well-being, community, care, empowerment, and justice for the poor easily fall into the background.

We are so culturally captive, even as contemporary Christians, that we urgently and desperately need to be saved.

While "self-salvation" is the motif of our contemporary culture, this form of recycling is mere repetition. We need to be saved from ourselves and from the worldliness of our world. Thus salvation needs to come to us from the Other, the great Other who in Christ took upon himself the sin of humanity to offer forgiveness, healing, and renewal.

A closed rational universe is simply our own construct. But an open universe both physically and spiritually sustained is the clear tale of the biblical narrative and is the taste of our own experience.

Nouwen informs us that "becoming the beloved is pulling the truth revealed to me from above down into the ordinariness of what I am."[70] That is the essence of our vocation as Christians, as humans.

That God created this world may shape my sense of stewardship for creation. That God offers redemption in Christ may shape my identity and the way I live in the world. May the Spirit as God's good gift empower me to live open to the mysterious, the supernatural, the empowering presence of God.

While much more could and should be said about the voice from beyond which may penetrate the very core of who I am and the way I order my life, the central message is clear. That we are saved by the great Other is no mere repetition but the in-breaking of the new. It opens us to the new world that only God can bring into being.

Resurrection
The penultimate human hope

IN OUR CONTEMPORARY WORLD, while there is some interest in space exploration, our major preoccupations are with our little globe. And for most of us our dominant concerns revolve around our own little lives: our living, loving, working, surviving, enjoying.

That there are great challenges facing us in our world is off the immediate radar screen for many. These challenges include the abject poverty of so many, and much closer to home, it is the tearing of the fabric of a tolerant and inclusive society and the re-emergence of old tribalisms.

That there are also challenges of a future that awaits us is part of the Christian story. A life now and a life to come have always been at the heart of Christianity. And throughout the pages of the Christian Testament runs the melody line of the resurrection as a belief, a hope, and a motif for living spirituality.

I live in the Christian hope that there is a life to come. This life, qualitatively different and therefore mysterious, is a life of fullness where the presence and goodness of God will determine and shape everything. Here God will be all in all.

This life to come, while qualitatively different from the one I am currently living, does offer some continuity. The life to come is a life of fullness in Christ, whose presence I already experience here. It is a life in the fullness of God, whose Spirit is already at work in me, the church, and in the world.

The life to come has to do with the resurrection of this body of mine, bringing it to wholeness and perfection. And it has to do with the healing of the nations, bringing all things into the peace and goodness of God.

The hope in the resurrection not only points us forward to what God will yet do. It also impacts us now. It is a key motif for Christian spirituality.

Henri Nouwen explains that "the resurrection is God's way of revealing to us that nothing that belongs to God will ever go to waste. What belongs to God will never get lost, not even our bodies!"[71]

Thus the life of faith lived in the now and the life of the world to come, while different, are not fundamentally disconnected or discontinuous. Because God in Christ has come among and has drawn near, God is both in the now and in the future. God is our present help and companion. And God is our future hope.

To live with this future, hope weaves our life with a continuous thread. A seamless tapestry is the work of our God. The God who was and is and is to come is the One who gathers up the whole of our lives.

All things, even the fragments of our lives, are gathered up in the renewing, healing, and restoring work of God. Thus all things can be placed in God's artistic hands, including the broken and wounded parts of our lives and our relationships.

Living in the light and hope of the life to come gives our present realities a perspective that is potentially revolutionary. The present seen in the light of God's future disempowers the present and breaks its mesmerizing power. The idols of the present stumble and fall in the light of the God's final unveiling and restoration. Thus we can live the present prophetically, having heard the whispers from the edge of eternity.

Henri Nouwen
A Brief Chronology

1932   January 24: Henri Josef Machiel born to Laurent and Maria Nouwen in the Dutch village of Nijkerk near Amsterdam.

1950   Enters seminary in Utrecht to train for the Roman Catholic priesthood.

1957   Ordained as priest in the archdiocese of Utrecht. Goes on to study psychology at the Catholic University of Nijmegen.

1964   Moves to the United States and becomes involved in clinical pastoral education and research at the Menninger Clinic in Topeka, Kansas.

1966   Appointed as visiting professor to the psychology department, University of Notre Dame, Indiana.

1968   Returns to The Netherlands and for the first two years teaches pastoral psychology and Christian spirituality to seminarians at the Pastoral Institute in Amsterdam.

1969   His first book, *Intimacy. Essays In Pastoral Psychology*, published.

1971   Works for a doctoral degree in theology at the University of Utrecht; publishes *Creative Ministry*.
Returns to the United States as professor of pastoral theology in the Divinity School, Yale University.

1972   *With Open Hands; Pray to Live* (reprinted in 1981 as *Thomas Merton: Contemplative Critic*); and *The Wounded Healer: Ministry in Contemporary Society* published.

1974   *Out of Solitude: Three Meditations on the Christian Life;* and
        Aging: The Fulfillment of Life, published.
        Spends some months in retreat at the Trappist Abbey of the
        Genesee in upstate New York; his reflections on this expe-
        rience published in 1976 as *The Genesee Diary: Report from
        a Trappist Monastery.*

1975   *Reaching Out: The Three Movements of the Spiritual Life*
        published.

1977   *The Living Reminder: Service and Prayer in Memory of Jesus
        Christ* published.

1979   *Clowning in Rome: Reflections on Solitude, Celibacy, Prayer,
        and Contemplation* published.

1980   *In Memoriam,* an extended reflection on the death of his
        mother, published.

1981   *The Way of the Heart; Making All Things New: An Initiation
        to the Spiritual Life;* and *A Cry for Mercy: Prayers from the
        Genesee* published.
        Resigns from Yale University and after a course in Spanish
        in Bolivia, joins the Maryknoll missionaries in Lima, Peru,
        for mission work with the poor.

1982   Returns to the United States after realizing that he isn't
        suited for this type of ministry.
        Compassion: A Reflection on the Christian Life; and *A Letter
        of Consolation* published.

1983   Begins teaching at Harvard University.
        Spends time in Mexico and Nicaragua, leading to a whirl-
        wind U.S. tour, pleading on behalf of the struggles of the
        people of Central and South America.
        Gracias! A Latin American Journal published.

1984 Makes a thirty-day retreat at the L'Arche Community in Trosly, France, leading to a growing interest in the work of Jean Vanier.

Travels to Guatemala to write the story of murdered missionary priest Stan Rother. This book is published in 1985 under the title *Love in a Fearful Land*.

1985 Leaves Harvard University to spend a year at Trosly as part of his growing conviction to live with and serve those with physical and intellectual disabilities. This journey is described in *The Road to Daybreak*, published in 1988.

1986 Becomes a resident priest at the Daybreak L'Arche Community in Toronto, Canada.

In the House of the Lord published. In the USA published as *Lifesigns*.

1987 *Behold the Beauty of the Lord* published.

1988 *Letters to Marc about Jesus* published. This is one of Nouwen's attempts to explain the Christian faith to a secular Western world. Nouwen goes through deep personal and spiritual crisis. His notes published in 1996 as *The Inner Voice of Love*.

1989 *Seeds of Hope; Heart Speaks to Heart: Three Prayers to Jesus; and In the Name of Jesus: Reflections on Christian Leadership* published.

1990 After a serious accident, Nouwen writes *Beyond the Mirror: Reflections on Death and Life. Walk with Jesus: Stations of the Cross* is also published.

1992 *Return of the Prodigal Son: A Meditation on Father, Brothers, and Sons* published.

1993 *Jesus and Mary: Finding Our Sacred Center* published. *Life of the Beloved: Spiritual Living in a Secular World* is also published. This is another attempt of Nouwen to share the gospel with a secular world.

1994   *Our Greatest Gift: A Meditation on Dying and Caring; With Burning Hearts: A Mediation on the Eucharistic Life;* and *Here and Now: Living in the Spirit* published.

1995   *The Path of Waiting; The Path of Freedom; The Path of Power;* and *the Path of Peace* published. This is republished in 2001 as *Finding My Way Home.*

1996   *Can You Drink This Cup?;* and *The Inner Voice of Love: A Journey through Anguish to Freedom* published.
September 21, Nouwen died of a heart attack in The Netherlands and on September 28 was buried in the Sacred Heart Cemetery near Toronto, Canada.

1997   *Adam: God's Beloved; Sabbatical Journey: The Final Year;* and *Bread for the Journey* published.

Notes

1 *The Inner Voice of Love*, p. 7.

2 *Sabbatical Journey*, p. 156.

3 *Finding My Way Home*, p. 64.

4 *The Genesee Diary*, p. 59.

5 *The Only Necessary Thing*, p. 44.

6 *Clowning in Rome*, p. 39.

7 *Beyond the Mirror*, p. 62.

8 *With Open Hands*, p. 13.

9 *Can You Drink the Cup?*,
   pp. 34-35.

10 *The Return of the Prodigal Son*,
   p. 53.

11 *Beyond the Mirror*, pp. 59, 62.

12 *Sabbatical Journey*, p. 134.

13 *The Way of the Heart*, p. 25.

14 *Here and Now*, p. 62.

15 *The Genesee Diary*, p. 68.

16 *Lifesigns*, p. 46.

17 *Clowning in Rome*, p. 52.

18 *Seeds of Hope*, p. 91.

19 *Intimacy*, p. 11.

20 *Adam*, p. 30.

21 *In the House of the Lord*, p. 27.

22 *The Only Necessary Thing*, p. 35.

23 *The Genesee Diary*, p. 20.

24 *Reaching Out*, p. 74.

25 *Life of the Beloved*, p. 118.

26 *Finding My Way Home*, p. 107.

27 *Sabbatical Journey*, p. 129.

28 *Clowning in Rome*, pp. 21-22.

29 *Making All Things New*, p. 49.

30 *In Memoriam*, p. 59.

31 *Heart Speaks to Heart*, p. 25.

32 *The Genesee Diary*, p. 217

33 *Heart Speaks to Heart*, pp. 23-24.

34 *In the Name of Jesus*, p. 41.

35 *Sabbatical Journey*, p. 127.

36 *Clowning in Rome*, p. 80.

37 *Beyond the Mirror*, p. 53.

38 *Our Greatest Gift*, p. 100.

39 *Lifesigns*, p. 45.

40 *Out of Solitude*, p. 34.

41 *Henri Nouwen: Writings Selected*,
   p. 104.

42 *Beyond the Mirror*, p. 72.

43 *Reaching Out*, p. 43.

44 *Clowning in Rome*, p. 25.

45 *The Inner Voice of Love*, p. xiii.

46 *The Way of the Heart*, p. 22.

47 *In the House of the Lord*, p. 61.

48 *Sabbatical Journey*, p. 7.

49 *The Road to Daybreak*, p. 81.

50 *Letters to Marc about Jesus*, p. 10.

51 *The Only Necessary Thing*, p. 176.

52 *With Open Hands*, p. 86.

53 *The Wounded Healer*, p. 19.

54 *The Genesee Diary*, pp. 112-113.

55 *In Memoriam*, p. 29.

56 *Heart Speaks to Heart*, p. 54.

57 *Seeds of Hope*, p. 10.

58 *The Return of the Prodigal Son*, p. 19.

59 *The Road to Daybreak*, p. 188.

60 *Life of the Beloved*, p. 78.

61 *The Only Necessary Thing*, p. 138.

62 *Making All Things New*, pp. 37, 42.

63 *The Genesee Diary*, p. 218.

64 *In the Name of Jesus*, p. 29.

65 *The Road to Daybreak*, p. 158.

66 *In the House of the Lord*, p. 57.

67 *Sabbatical Journey*, p. 100.

68 *The Only Necessary Thing*, p. 36.

69 *Clowning in Rome*, p. 46.

70 *Henri Nouwen: Writings Selected*, p. 30.

71 *Our Greatest Gift*, pp. 116-117.

Bibliography
Works by Henri J.M. Nouwen

Adam: God's Beloved. Maryknoll, NY: Orbis Books, 1997.

Aging: The Fulfillment of Life (with Walter Gaffney). New York: Doubleday, 1974.

Behold the Beauty of the Lord: Praying with Icons. Notre Dame, IN: Ave Maria Press, 1987.

Beyond the Mirror: Reflections on Death and Life. New York: Crossroads, 1991.

Bread for the Journey: A Daybook of Wisdom and Faith. New York: HarperCollins, 1997.

Can you Drink the Cup? Notre Dame, IN: Ave Maria Press, 1996.

Clowning in Rome: Reflections on Solitude, Celibacy, Prayer, and Contemplation. New York: Image Books, 1979.

Compassion: A Reflection of the Christian Life (with J.M. McNeil and D.P. Morrison). London: Darton, Longman and Todd, 1982.

Creative Ministry: Beyond Professionalism in Teaching, Preaching, Counseling, Organizing, and Celebrating. New York: Doubleday, 1971.

A Cry for Mercy: Prayers from the Genesee. Dublin: Gill & Macmillan, 1982.

Finding My Way Home: Pathways to Life and the Spirit. New York: Crossroad, 2001.

The Genesee Diary: Report from a Trappist Monastery. New York: Doubleday, 1976.

Gracias! A Latin American Journal. New York: Harper & Row, 1983.

Heart Speaks to Heart: Three Prayers to Jesus. Notre Dame, IN: Ave Maria Press, 1989.

Henri Nouwen: Writings Selected (Introduction by Robert A. Jonas). Maryknoll, NY: Orbis Books, 1998.

Here and Now: Living in the Spirit. New York: Crossroad, 1994.

The Inner Voice of Love: A Journey Through Anguish to Freedom. New York: Doubleday, 1996.

In the House of the Lord. London: Darton, Longman and Todd, 1986.

In Memoriam. Notre Dame, IN: Ave Maria Press, 1980.

In the Name of Jesus: Reflections on Christian Leadership. New York: Crossroad, 1989.

Intimacy: Pastoral Psychological Essays. Notre Dame, IN: Fides/Claretian, 1969.

Jesus and Mary: Finding Our Sacred Center. Cincinnati, OH: St. Anthony Messenger Press, 1993.

Letters to Marc about Jesus. London: Darton, Longman and Todd, 1988.

A Letter of Consolation. Dublin: Gill & Macmillan, 1983.

Life of the Beloved: Spiritual Living in a Secular World. New York: Crossroad, 1993.

Lifesigns: Intimacy, Fecundity, and Ecstasy in Christian Perspective. New York: Image Books, 1989.

The Living Reminder: Service and Prayer in Memory of Jesus Christ. New York: Seabury, 1977.

Love in a Fearful Land: A Guatemalan Story. Notre Dame, IN: Ave Maria Press, 1985.

Making All Things New: An Invitation to the Spiritual Life. San Francisco: Harper & Row, 1981.

The Only Necessary Thing: Living a Prayerful Life (compiled and edited by Wendy Wilson Greer). New York: Crossroad, 1999.

Our Greatest Gift: A Meditation on Dying and Caring. London: Hodder & Stoughton, 1994.

Out of Solitude: Three Meditations on the Christian Life. Notre Dame, IN: Ave Maria Press, 1974.

Pray to Live. Notre Dame, IN: Fides, 1972.

Reaching Out: The Three Movements of the Spiritual Life. New York: Doubleday, 1975.

The Return of the Prodigal Son: A Story of Homecoming. London: Darton, Longman and Todd, 1994.

The Road to Daybreak. A Spiritual Journey. New York: Doubleday, 1988.

Sabbatical Journey: The Diary of His Final Year. New York: Crossroad, 1998.

Seeds of Hope (edited and introduced by Robert Durback). London: Darton, Longman and Todd, 1989.

Thomas Merton: Contemplative Critic. New York: Harper & Row, 1981.

Walk with Jesus: Stations of the Cross. Maryknoll, NY: Orbis, 1990.

The Way of the Heart: Desert Spirituality and Contemporary Ministry. Minneapolis: Seabury Press, 1981.

With Burning Hearts: A Meditation on the Eucharistic Life. Maryknoll, NY: Orbis Books, 1994.

With Open Hands. Notre Dame, IN: Ave Maria Press, 1995 (first published, 1972).

The Wounded Healer: Ministry in Contemporary Society. New York: Image Books, 1979.

About Paraclete Press

Who We Are

Paraclete Press is an ecumenical publisher of books and recordings on Christian spirituality. Our publishing represents a full expression of Christian belief and practice—from Catholic to Evangelical, from Protestant to Orthodox.

Paraclete Press is the publishing arm of the Community of Jesus, an ecumenical monastic community in the Benedictine tradition. As such, we are uniquely positioned in the marketplace without connection to a large corporation and with informal relationships to many branches and denominations of faith.

We like it best when people buy our books from booksellers, our partners in successfully reaching as wide an audience as possible.

What We Are Doing
Books

Paraclete Press publishes books that show the richness and depth of what it means to be Christian. Although Benedictine spirituality is at the heart of all that we do, we publish books that reflect the Christian experience across many cultures, time periods, and houses of worship.

We publish books that nourish the vibrant life of the church and its people— books about spiritual practice, formation, history, ideas, and customs.

We have several different series of books within Paraclete Press, including the bestselling Living Library series of modernized classic texts; *A Voice from the Monastery*—giving voice to men and women monastics about what it means to live a spiritual life today; award-winning literary faith fiction; and books that explore Judaism and Islam and discover how these faiths inform Christian thought and practice.

Recordings

From Gregorian chant to contemporary American choral works, our music recordings celebrate the richness of sacred choral music through the centuries. Paraclete is proud to distribute the recordings of the internationally acclaimed choir Gloriæ Dei Cantores, who have been praised for their "rapt and fathomless spiritual intensity" by *American Record Guide*, and the Gloriæ Dei Cantores Schola, which specializes in the study and performance of Gregorian chant. Paraclete is also the exclusive North American distributor of the recordings of the Monastic Choir of St. Peter's Abbey in Solesmes, France, long considered to be a leading authority on Gregorian chant performance.

Learn more about us at our website:
www.paracletepress.com, or call us toll-free at
1-800-451-5006.

If you liked *The Seeking Heart,* you may also enjoy:

The Wet Engine
Brian Doyle
ISBN: 1-55725-405-2
170 pages
$17.95, Hardcover

"Every creature on earth has approximately two billion heartbeats to spend in a lifetime. You can spend them slowly, like a tortoise, and live to be two hundred years old, or you can spend them fast, like a hummingbird, and live to be two years old."

This startling, genuinely unique book moves like a freight train through the scientific, emotional, literary, philosophical, and spiritual understandings of the heart—from cardiology to courage, from love letters and pop songs to Jesus. The torment of Doyle's own infant son's heart surgery is the thread weaving the strands together, but the wisdom is for every person who seeks a more passionate life, in touch with the heart of God.

Incandescence
365 Readings with Women Mystics
Carmen Acevedo Butcher
Foreword by Phyllis Tickle
ISBN: 1-55725-418-4
296 pages
$16.95, Trade Paper

Turn to any page in this beautiful collection and you will discover the women mystics of Christian tradition. These fascinating women show us a picture of a tender, nurturing, forgiving God who is as intimate as our own breath. *Incandescence* offers fresh translations from the writings of famous and not-so-famous mystics—Julian of Norwich, Mechthild of Magdeburg, Catherine of Siena, Hildegard of Bingen, Gertrude of Helfta, Margery Kempe, and others.

Available from most booksellers or through Paraclete Press:
www.paracletepress.com; 1-800-451-5006.
Try your local bookstore first.